A Cartoon History of the District of Columbia

by Patrick M. Reynolds

Published by

The Red Rose Studio
Willow Street, PA 17584

Contents

The page numbers are placed on drawings of famous structures and monuments in the DC area.

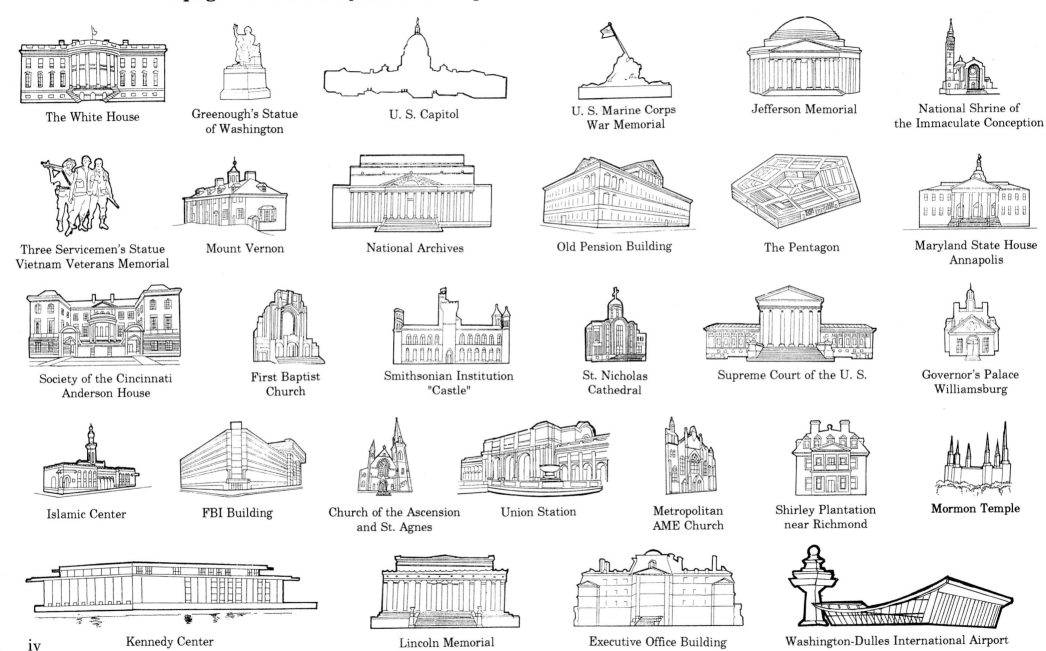

The White House

Greenough's Statue
of Washington

U. S. Capitol

U. S. Marine Corps
War Memorial

Jefferson Memorial

National Shrine of
the Immaculate Conception

Three Servicemen's Statue
Vietnam Veterans Memorial

Mount Vernon

National Archives

Old Pension Building

The Pentagon

Maryland State House
Annapolis

Society of the Cincinnati
Anderson House

First Baptist
Church

Smithsonian Institution
"Castle"

St. Nicholas
Cathedral

Supreme Court of the U. S.

Governor's Palace
Williamsburg

Islamic Center

FBI Building

Church of the Ascension
and St. Agnes

Union Station

Metropolitan
AME Church

Shirley Plantation
near Richmond

Mormon Temple

Kennedy Center

Lincoln Memorial

Executive Office Building

Washington-Dulles International Airport

Introduction

The stories in this book are reproductions of an illustrated feature called **Flashbacks**. Since October 13, 1991, **Flashbacks** has appeared every Sunday in the comics section of **The Washington Post.** Other newspapers that carry **Flashbacks** are the **Erie** (PA) **Times-News, Greensburg** (PA) **Tribune-Review, Harrisburg** (PA) **Patriot-News,** and **Pottsville** (PA) **Republican.** Many different topics from various time periods are covered in **Flashbacks** but, for this book, I have selected those stories that deal with the early days of Washington.

This is illustrated history-telling where the most difficult task is to visualize what something looked like without the benefit of paintings, photos, or drawings from two centuries ago. Most of the personalities in this book were caricatured from their portraits. However, some people such as Pierre L'Enfant, Stephen Hallett, and George Hadfield never had their portraits painted. In those instances, I made up their likeness.

Special Thanks

The most fun in writing and illustrating history is doing the research and meeting the wonderful people who have helped me along the way. First and foremost are the volunteers in the library of the Historical Society of Washington, DC who provided information and graphics on a variety of subjects. For the sequence on the construction of the U. S. Capitol, I was aided by William Allen, Architectural Historian of the U. S. Capitol. Dr. Barbara A. Wolanin, Curator of the Office of the Architect of the Capitol and her staff helped with the *Statue of Freedom* atop the dome. For details about Benjamin Banneker and pictures of old surveying instruments, I am thankful to Wylene Burch, Director of the Howard County (MD) Center of African American Culture in Columbia, MD.

I also want to commend the Maryland Historical Society in Baltimore for displaying my **Flashbacks** series on Benjamin Latrobe in their special exhibition on *The World of Benjamin Henry Latrobe.*

Section One
The Moving Capital

These are the cities which served as the capital of the United States of America. Early on, Congress was running away from the British, later they were being chased by irate citizens. They finally selected a location that was both difficult to invade and even harder to find--Washington, D.C.

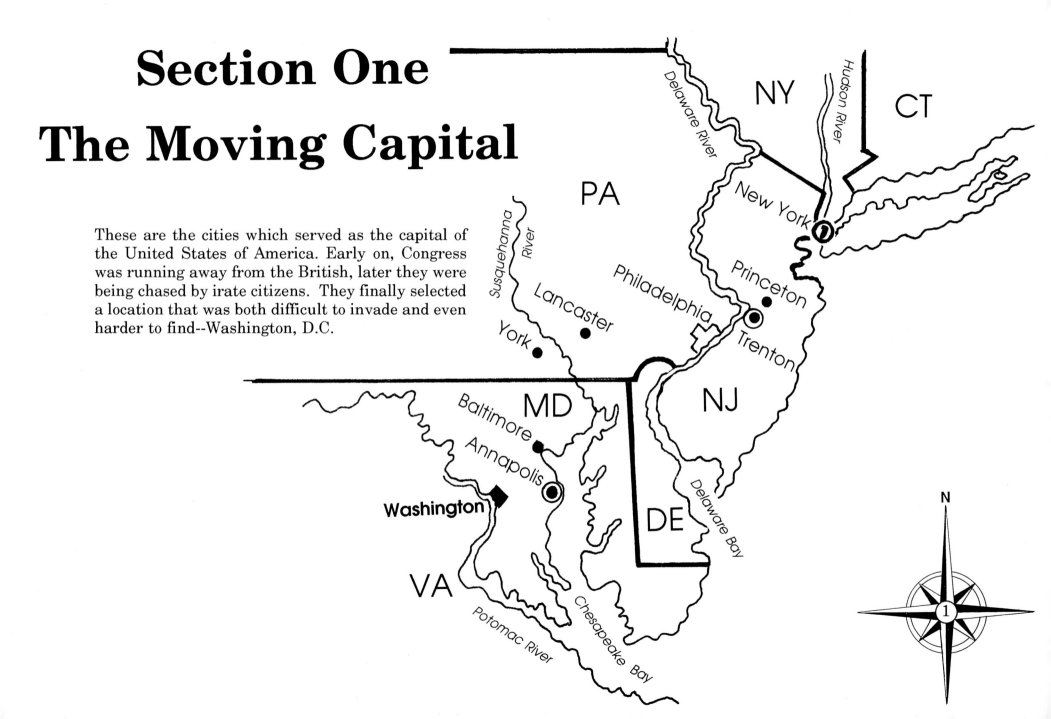

Two centuries before the capital of the United States was placed on the Potomac River, another seat of government was located in the area. The Patawomeck Indians had their capital town on Aquia Creek, a tributary of the Potomac in Stafford County, Virginia.

DURING THE 16th AND 17th CENTURIES, A STRONG TRIBE CALLED THE PATAWOMECK LIVED ALONG A RIVER WHICH BORE THEIR NAME. PATAWOMECK CAME TO BE SPELLED **POTOMAC**, SUPPOSEDLY AN ALGONQUIAN PHRASE MEANING "TO BRING AGAIN; THEY GO AND COME."

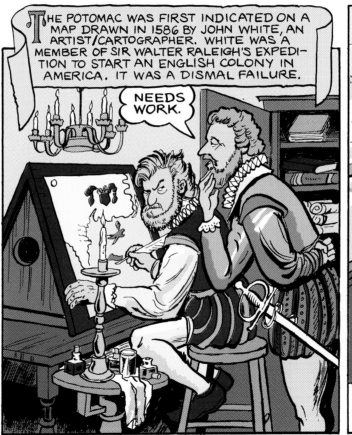

THE POTOMAC WAS FIRST INDICATED ON A MAP DRAWN IN 1586 BY JOHN WHITE, AN ARTIST/CARTOGRAPHER. WHITE WAS A MEMBER OF SIR WALTER RALEIGH'S EXPEDITION TO START AN ENGLISH COLONY IN AMERICA. IT WAS A DISMAL FAILURE.

NEEDS WORK.

THE FIRST DOCUMENTED EXPLORATION OF THE POTOMAC WAS MADE BY CAPTAIN JOHN SMITH IN JUNE, 1608. HE SAILED UPSTREAM AS FAR AS LITTLE FALLS, NEXT TO WHAT IS NOW WASHINGTON, D.C.

The closest thing the thirteen colonies had to a Federal government was the Continental Congress. The first important document produced by this organization was the Declaration of Independence.

Whenever the Congress changed meeting places, the delegates took the parchment with them. To get a tour of the cities that served as the capital of the United States, just follow the Declaration of Independence.

The Declaration of Independence

America's most famous document has traveled on just about every mode of transportation except the airplane.

WAS ADOPTED BY ALL THE AMERICAN COLONIES EXCEPT NEW YORK ON JULY 4, 1776. ON THAT DAY THE ONLY PEOPLE WHO SIGNED A PRINTED COPY OF IT WERE JOHN HANCOCK, PRESIDENT OF THE CONTINENTAL CONGRESS, AND CHARLES THOMSON, SECRETARY OF THE CONGRESS.

TWO WEEKS LATER, CONGRESS HIRED TIMOTHY MATLACK, A PHILADELPHIA ARTIST, TO "ENGROSS" THE DECLARATION. HURRYING TO FINISH IT BY AUGUST 2nd, MATLACK MADE SOME SPELLING ERRORS THAT WERE NEVER CORRECTED.

UNITED STATES BEGINS WITH A CAPITAL "U."

THERE'S ONLY ONE "T" IN BRITISH!

IN LATE JULY, NEW YORK FINALLY VOTED IN FAVOR OF THE DECLARATION & SENT FOUR SIGNERS. ON AUGUST 2nd, THE DELEGATES LINED UP TO SIGN MATLACK'S PARCHMENT. EVENTUALLY 56 MEN WOULD SIGN IT.

BEFORE THE END OF THE YEAR, THE TRAVELS OF THE DECLARATION OF INDEPENDENCE HAD BEGUN. WITH THE BRITISH CLOSING IN ON PHILADELPHIA, CONGRESS MOVED TO A BUILDING ON BALTIMORE AND LIBERTY STREETS IN **BALTIMORE, MD.** THE DECLARATION WAS CARRIED THERE IN A BAGGAGE WAGON.

THE DECLARATION CAME BACK TO **PHILADELPHIA** WITH CONGRESS IN MARCH, 1777.

The British decided to occupy the colonial capital of Philadelphia in the fall of 1777. General George Washington tried to stop them at Brandywine and Germantown, but General Howe out-foxed him and moved into Philadelphia in October. There were several small skirmishes on the outskirts of the city but hostilities ceased with the onset of winter. At the suggestion of General "Mad" Anthony Wayne, Washington set up camp at a place called Valley Forge.

The Moving Declaration

IN SEPTEMBER, 1777, THE BRITISH WERE ABOUT TO OCCUPY PHILADELPHIA, SO CONGRESS FLED WESTWARD, TAKING THE DECLARATION OF INDEPENDENCE WITH THEM. THEY RECONVENED FOR ONE DAY IN LANCASTER, PA.

NEXT, THE GOVERNMENT AND THE DECLARATION CROSSED THE SUSQUEHANNA RIVER AND MADE YORK, PA THE CAPITAL FOR THE FOLLOWING EIGHT MONTHS.

THE DECLARATION WENT BACK TO INDEPENDENCE HALL IN PHILLY IN JUNE, 1778, AND STAYED THERE UNTIL...

JUNE, 1783, WHEN DISGRUNTLED VETERANS CONVERGED ON PHILADELPHIA DEMANDING THEIR UNPAID WAGES FOR FIGHTING THE REVOLUTIONARY WAR.

TO AVOID TROUBLE, CONGRESS GRABBED THEIR SUITCASES AND THE DECLARATION AND HIGH-TAILED IT TO NASSAU HALL AT PRINCETON, NEW JERSEY.

IN NOVEMBER, THE PARCHMENT ACCOMPANIED CONGRESS TO THE STATE HALL IN ANNAPOLIS, MD.

THEN, ON TO THE OLD STONE CHURCH AT TRENTON, NEW JERSEY IN 1784.

A YEAR LATER CONGRESS AND THE DECLARATION TOOK UP RESIDENCE IN NEW YORK'S CITY HALL.

The veterans' beef was with the government of Pennsylvania and it was finally mediated by "Mad" Anthony Wayne. Since Pennsylvania was virtually broke, the state gave land to the veterans. That is how the northwestern part of the Commonwealth was settled.

5

At the close of the Revolution, Maryland offered to cede Annapolis as the Federal Capital. During the negotiations for a permanent site, it was resolved in 1783 to alternate the capital between Annapolis and Trenton.

Meanwhile, the law of the land was the Articles of Confederation which proved weak and ineffective. So, in 1787, the Convention of the States was held in Philadelphia and they created the Constitution.

What Ever Happened to the Declaration of Independence?

THE CONSTITUTION OF THE UNITED STATES WENT INTO EFFECT IN 1789 AND THE DECLARATION OF INDEPENDENCE WAS IN THE NATION'S CAPITOL, NEW YORK'S CITY HALL AT BROAD AND WALL STREETS.

CONGRESS PASSED A LAW WHICH PLACED THE DECLARATION IN THE CUSTODY OF THE SECRETARY OF STATE. AT THE TIME HE WAS ONE OF THE DOCUMENT'S AUTHORS, **THOMAS JEFFERSON.**

A YEAR LATER PHILADELPHIA AGAIN BECAME CAPITAL OF THE U.S. AND THE DECLARATION WENT THERE FOR A TEN-YEAR STAY. MEANWHILE, FEDERAL CITY, NOW WASHINGTON, D.C. WAS UNDER CONSTRUCTION.

THE FEDERAL GOVERNMENT MOVED TO WASHINGTON IN 1800 AND THE DECLARATION WAS LITERALLY *SHIPPED* THERE.

IN THE SUMMER OF 1814 THE BRITISH WERE ABOUT TO ATTACK WASHINGTON, SO SECRETARY OF STATE JAMES MONROE CARRIED THE DECLARATION TO VIRGINIA AND HID IT IN ED PATTERSON'S BARN.

NEXT, IT WAS REMOVED TO REV. LITTLEJOHN'S HOME IN LEESBURG.

BACK IN WASHINGTON THE DECLARATION MOVED TO WHEREVER THE STATE DEPARTMENT MOVED. THEN, IN 1841, SECRETARY OF STATE DANIEL WEBSTER PUT IT ON DISPLAY IN THE NEW PATENT OFFICE BLDG. AT 7th & G STREETS.

FOR THE NEXT 35 YEARS IT HUNG THERE, UNPROTECTED FROM THE SUN AND CHANGES IN TEMPERATURE.

Note: Whenever the Declaration was moved, it was always rolled from top to bottom. This damaged some of the signatures at the bottom of the document because the delegates signed in ink and the parchment does not absorb ink. Once ink dries, it flakes easily.

Besides its exposure to the sun, experts believe that something else had damaged the Declaration. Back in 1823, Secretary of State John Quincy Adams decided to make copies of the famous document. Since the camera had not been invented yet, here's what they did. The Declaration was first dusted with powder. Then, moist paper was pressed against the parchment and an exact reverse copy was lifted from the original. This caused some of the ink to be loosened. At any rate, Adams got his copies printed and they were distributed throughout the country.

The Further Travels of the Parchment

IN 1876 PRESIDENT U.S. GRANT PERMITTED THE DECLARATION OF INDEPENDENCE TO BE TAKEN BY TRAIN TO THE AMERICAN CENTENNIAL EXPOSITION IN PHILADELPHIA.

MANY PEOPLE WHO VIEWED IT WERE APPALLED BY ITS POOR CONDITION.

AFTER THE EXPOSITION, THE DECLARATION WAS RETURNED TO WASHINGTON AND EXHIBITED IN THE NEW STATE, WAR, AND NAVY BUILDING. IT WAS A GOOD DECISION BECAUSE THE PATENT OFFICE BUILDING, WHERE IT HAD BEEN DISPLAYED, BURNED DOWN A FEW WEEKS LATER.

MEANWHILE CONGRESS APPOINTED A COMMITTEE TO FIND SOME WAYS TO RESTORE THE DOCUMENT.

FIVE YEARS LATER THE COMMITTEE REPORTED TO CONGRESS.

IT IS NOT EXPEDIENT TO RESTORE THE DOCUMENT. IT SHOULD BE STORED IN A DARK PLACE.

NOTHING WAS DONE. IT REMAINED ON DISPLAY FOR TEN MORE YEARS IN THE STATE, WAR, AND NAVY BUILDING WHICH IS NOW THE EXECUTIVE OFFICE BLDG.

IN 1894 PRESIDENT GROVER CLEVELAND HAD THE PARCHMENT LOCKED IN A SAFE. THE PUBLIC WOULD NOT SEE IT AGAIN FOR ALMOST THIRTY YEARS.

The page number is on the Executive Office Building at 17th Street and Pennsylvania Avenue, NW. This used to be the State, War, and Navy Building which housed the Declaration of Independence from 1877 to 1894.

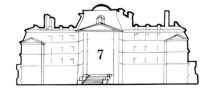

A committee appointed by the Secretary of State made the following report on April 21, 1920: "We find that the parchment is still strong, pliable, and without signs of deterioration. We believe that the fading can go no further. We see no reason why the original document should not be exhibited if the parchment be laid between two sheets of glass, hermetically sealed at the edges, and exposed only to diffused light."

THE DOCUMENT SHRINE

HEEDING THE ADVICE OF SECRETARY OF STATE CHARLES EVAN HUGHES, PRESIDENT WARREN G. HARDING ISSUED AN ORDER THAT TRANSFERRED CUSTODY OF THE DECLARATION OF INDEPENDENCE FROM THE STATE DEPT. TO THE LIBRARY OF CONGRESS ON SEPTEMBER 20, 1921.

THE PARCHMENT WAS TAKEN OUT OF A SAFE, PLACED IN A MAIL TRUCK, DRIVEN TO THE LIBRARY OF CONGRESS AND LOCKED IN ANOTHER SAFE.

WITHIN A FEW WEEKS CONGRESS FUNDED A SHRINE FOR THE DECLARATION *AND* CONSTITUTION IN THE LIBRARY'S *GREAT HALL.*

ON FEB. 28, 1924, PRESIDENT AND MRS. CALVIN COOLIDGE DEDICATED THE SHRINE.

DURING WORLD WAR II (1941-44) THE DOCUMENTS WERE STORED AT FORT KNOX, KY.

AFTER THE WAR THE DECLARATION AND THE CONSTITUTION WERE RETURNED TO THEIR SHRINE IN THE LIBRARY OF CONGRESS.

IN 1951 THE DOCUMENTS WERE SEALED WITHIN AN INERT HELIUM GAS ENVIRONMENT IN SPECIAL GLASS AND BRONZE CASES.

ON DEC. 13, 1952 THE CASES WERE MOVED TO THEIR PRESENT HOME IN THE NATIONAL ARCHIVES BLDG.

8

When the Declaration and Constitution were shipped to Fort Knox, they were placed in a special bronze container then sealed with wire and lead. The container was put aboard a train bound for Louisville, Kentucky.

The documents arrived at Fort Knox on December 26, 1941. While at the fort, the Declaration was examined from time to time by a scientist and a conservator to make certain that no further harm had come to it.

Brigadier General Stoyte O. Ross, Commanding General of the Headquarters Command of the U. S. Air Force was in charge of the transfer of the Declaration of Independence and the Constitution. He led the parade of military vehicles along with men and women of all the armed forces to the Archives Building and delivered the documents to Dr. Wayne C. Grover, Archivist of the United States.

Parade of the Parchments

ON DECEMBER 13, 1952, THE DECLARATION OF INDEPENDENCE AND THE U.S. CONSTITUTION WERE PACKED IN FLAT, WOODEN **BOXES**, CARRIED OUT OF THE LIBRARY OF CONGRESS, AND PLACED ABOARD A MARINE CORPS ARMORED VEHICLE.

THE SHORT RIDE TO THEIR PRESENT SHRINE IN THE NATIONAL ARCHIVES BUILDING WAS AN ELABORATE PARADE CONSISTING OF BRASS BANDS AND MEMBERS OF ALL THE ARMED FORCES. THE PARCHMENTS WERE ESCORTED BY TWO ARMY TANKS, BUT ONE OF THEM BROKE DOWN EARLY IN THE PARADE.

TWO DAYS LATER PRESIDENT HARRY S. TRUMAN AND CHIEF JUSTICE FREDERICK M. VINSON FORMALLY DEDICATED THE NEW SHRINE OF AMERICA'S MOST PRECIOUS DOCUMENTS.

NOW, THE DECLARATION, CONSTITUTION, AND BILL OF RIGHTS TRAVEL EVERY DAY.

THIS CUT-AWAY VIEW SHOWS THAT THEY ARE HOUSED ATOP AN ELEVATOR.

AT NIGHT THE DOCU-MENTS ARE LOWERED TWENTY FEET INTO A VAULT.

Despite their preoccupation with creating courts and executive departments, raising revenues, and passing the Bill of Rights, many Congressmen found time to wheel and deal for a permanent national capital.

THE CAPITAL DEBATE

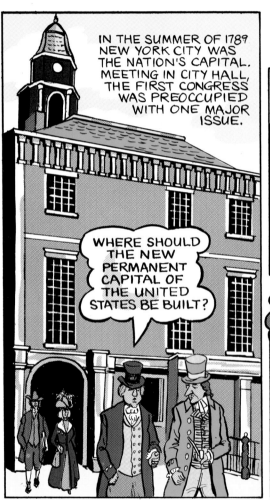

IN THE SUMMER OF 1789 NEW YORK CITY WAS THE NATION'S CAPITAL. MEETING IN CITY HALL, THE FIRST CONGRESS WAS PREOCCUPIED WITH ONE MAJOR ISSUE.

WHERE SHOULD THE NEW PERMANENT CAPITAL OF THE UNITED STATES BE BUILT?

ONE THING WE'RE ALL AGREED UPON— IT SHOULD BE FAR OUT IN THE COUNTRY...

AWAY FROM COMMERCIAL *INTERESTS WHO TRY TO INFLUENCE THE DELEGATES IN THE LARGER CITIES.

...GOT A MINUTE, SENATOR?

*TODAY THEY ARE CALLED LOBBYISTS.

MOST OF THE SOUTHERN POLITICIANS WANTED THE NEW CAPITAL TO BE NEAR GEORGETOWN ON THE POTOMAC RIVER.

MY COLLEAGUES FROM THE NEW ENGLAND STATES WOULD RATHER **SECEDE** THAN **BOIL** IN THE SOUTH!

SOME NORTHERN CONGRESSMEN PREFERRED A SITE ON THE DELAWARE RIVER NEAR **TRENTON, NJ.**

SENATORS SCOTT AND MACLAY OF PENNSYLVANIA PUSHED HARD FOR A SPOT NEAR WRIGHT'S FERRY ON THE **SUSQUEHANNA RIVER...**

WHICH PROMPTED THIS REACTION FROM THE SOUTHERNERS,

WE'LL **SECEDE** SOONER THAN **FREEZE** IN THE NORTH

The Common Council of New York City raised $65,000 to transform the old city hall at Wall and Nassau Streets into an ornate Federal Hall where Congress would convene. Pierre L'Enfant, a military engineer from France who fought in the American Revolution, redesigned and renovated the structure.

The National Debt

No one believed the capital would stay in New York very long. A fever epidemic struck New York in August, 1798, and Common Council ordered churches to stop tolling their bells during funerals for fear of scaring Congress out of the city.

THE PRESENT LOCATION OF OUR NATIONAL CAPITAL GREW OUT OF A SQUABBLE OVER FEDERAL FINANCES.

IT ALL STARTED IN 1789 AT NEW YORK CITY WHICH, AT THE TIME, WAS THE CAPITAL OF THE (ORIGINAL THIRTEEN) UNITED STATES.

BY SEPTEMBER, THE CONGRESSIONAL DEBATE OVER WHERE TO LOCATE THE NEW NATIONAL CAPITAL WAS REPLACED BY A MORE PRESSING ISSUE—THE NATIONAL DEBT.

CONGRESS HAS DECIDED TO LET THE NEW SECRETARY OF THE TREASURY FIGURE OUT HOW TO PAY IT.

AMERICA'S **FIRST** SECRETARY OF THE TREASURY WAS A 34 YEAR OLD NEW YORK BANKER NAMED **ALEXANDER HAMILTON.**

I HAVE A TWO-PART **PLAN!**

FIRST, THE FEDERAL GOVERNMENT WILL **BORROW** MONEY TO PAY THE DEBT....

AND PAY OFF THE LOAN WITH **TAXES** ON IMPORTED GOODS AND DOMESTIC **WHISKEY.**

CONGRESS QUICKLY APPROVED THE FIRST PART.

AYE! AYE!

THE SECOND PART WAS TROUBLE.

CONGRESS WILL PAY THE DEBTS WHICH THE STATES INCURRED FIELDING THEIR MILITIAS IN THE REVOLUTIONARY WAR.

WHA-GRP

WE SOUTHERNAHS PAID OUR DEBTS, AN' WE'RE NOT ABOUT T' LET THE NORTH OUT OF PAYIN' THEIRS!

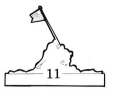

Representative Richard Bland Lee of Virginia voiced the basic argument for placing the capital on the Potomac. He explained that the river was situated midway between Massachusetts and Georgia, then the extent of the United States. Its southern location had "a most salubrious climate.

HAMILTON'S IDEA

IN 1789 TREASURY SECRETARY ALEXANDER HAMILTON INTRODUCED THE ASSUMPTION BILL TO CONGRESS IN NEW YORK CITY, THEN CAPITAL OF THE U.S.

THE FEDERAL GOVERNMENT WILL ASSUME *(PAY OFF)* THE DEBTS INCURRED BY THE STATES DURING THE REVOLUTIONARY WAR.

THE NORTHERN STATES WERE HAVING A HARD TIME PAYING THEIR WAR DEBTS BECAUSE THEY HAD FIELDED LARGE ARMIES AND NAVIES.

MOST OF THE SUPPLIES, AMMUNITION, AND RATIONS CAME FROM MILLS AND FARMS IN THE NORTHERN STATES.

SEND THE BILL TO THE STATE OF NEW JERSEY.

ON THE OTHER HAND, THE SOUTHERN STATES HAD SMALL POPULATIONS, SMALL ARMIES, FEW MAJOR BATTLES, AND SMALLER DEBTS WHICH THEY WERE ABLE TO PAY RATHER QUICKLY.

NEVERTHELESS, THE SOUTH AIN'T GONNA CHIP IN T' PAY THOSE YANKEES' DEBTS.

HAMILTON WAS DETERMINED TO HAVE HIS WAY.

I WANT A **STRONG** CENTRAL GOVERNMENT. IF THE FEDERAL GOVERNMENT PAYS THE STATES' DEBTS...

THE STATES WILL BECOME DEPENDENT ON FEDERAL MONEY. THIS WILL MAKE THE STATES LESS POWERFUL.

DEADLOCKED OVER HAMILTON'S ASSUMPTION BILL, CONGRESS WENT BACK TO ARGUING ABOUT WHERE TO BUILD THE NEW NATIONAL CAPITAL.

DOWN SOUTH! UP NORTH!

THIS GAVE MR. HAMILTON AN IDEA.

I **DON'T CARE** WHERE THEY PUT THE CAPITAL. *BUT,* WHY NOT **TRADE VOTES** FOR THE...

LOCATION OF THE CAPITAL IN EXCHANGE FOR VOTES ON MY ASSUMPTION BILL?

12

ennsylvania delegates were scrambling to get the capital
oved to their state as soon as possible. Meanwhile, James
adison a Congressman from Virginia, was happy to keep
e location of the capital off the busy Congressional agenda.

NE DAY IN THE SPRING OF 1790, TREASURY SECRETARY
LEXANDER HAMILTON BUMPED INTO THE SECRETARY
F STATE, THOMAS JEFFERSON, OUTSIDE PRESIDENT
ASHINGTON'S RESIDENCE AT 39 **BROADWAY** IN NEW
ORK CITY, THEN THE NATION'S CAPITAL. THEY PACED BACK
ND FORTH FOR A HALF HOUR DISCUSSING MAJOR ISSUES.

TOM, IT'S **VITAL** THAT CONGRESS PASS THE ASSUMPTION BILL WHICH WILL ENABLE THE FEDERAL GOVERNMENT TO PAY THE STATES' DEBTS.

COME DINE AT MY PLACE **TOMORROW** NIGHT... WE'LL SEE WHAT WE CAN WORK OUT.

THE CAPITAL DEAL

JEFFERSON ALSO INVITED TWO VIRGINIA CONGRESSMEN, AND THE GROUP MADE A DEAL.

VIRGINIA WILL VOTE FOR THE FEDERAL ASSUMPTION OF THE STATES' DEBTS.

MISTAH HAM'LTON ???

IN **RETURN**, I'LL GET NORTHERN SUPPORT FOR A **SOUTHERN** CAPITAL.

BOTH SIDES KEPT THEIR WORD. AS A RESULT, THE UNITED STATES GOT WASHINGTON, D.C. AS ITS CAPITAL AND...

THE UNITED STATES OF AMERICA
10 · TEN · 10
HAMILTON
TEN DOLLARS

THE NATIONAL DEBT.

After Jefferson and Hamilton reached the agreement
described here, the only way that Congress could muster
enough votes for a new capital was to split its sessions
between Trenton in the North and Annapolis in the South.

Payback time for the Capital Compromise came in 1794 when Congress
passed a tax on whiskey. Farmers in western Pennsylvania reacted
violently by starting the famous Whiskey Rebellion. President
Washington activated the militias of Maryland and New Jersey to put
down this insurrection.

13

Section Two

Plans and Preparations

Every aspect of establishing a city on the Potomac was wrought with headaches: selecting the site, acquiring the land, designing the city, and straightening out the sabotaged land survey. All would have gone smoothly except for President Washington's worst appointees--the Capital District Commissioners.

15

Once the Northern and Southern politicians agreed that the Federal government would pay the states' Revolutionary War debts, they went to work on a bill, or act, that would establish the new, permanent capital of the United States of America.

THE RESIDENCE ACT,

WHICH DECIDED THE GENERAL LOCATION OF THE U.S. CAPITAL, BECAME LAW IN 1790. IT ALLOWED THE PRESIDENT TO CHOOSE THE EXACT SPOT ON THE POTOMAC RIVER...

ANYWHERE BETWEEN THE MOUTH OF THE EASTERN BRANCH AND THE CONOCOCHEAGUE CREEK, SOME 70 MILES UPSTREAM.

NEXT, PRESIDENT WASHINGTON TOURED THE POTOMAC VALLEY. HERE, HE STOPS AT THE GREAT FALLS.

MARYLAND

POTOMAC

SITE EVENTUALLY SELECTED

EASTERN BRANCH (NOW, THE ANACOSIA RIVER)

POTOMAC RIVER

VIRGINIA

PRINCE GEORGE'S COUNTY

CHARLES COUNTY

* NEAR HAGERSTOWN, MD.

THE BEST LOCATION WOULD BE NEAR THE PORTS OF ALEXANDRIA, VIRGINIA AND GEORGETOWN, MARYLAND.

B'SIDES, IT'S FAR ENOUGH FROM THE ATLANTIC TO BE SAFE FROM ATTACK BY AN ENEMY NAVY.

NOW WE HAVE TO DEAL WITH THE FARMERS WHO OWN THE LAND WHERE THE CAPITAL WILL BE. FORTUNATELY, I KNOW MOST OF THEM.

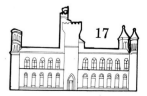

17

GETTING THE LAND

TO BUILD WASHINGTON, D.C. WAS A DELICATE MATTER BECAUSE THE FEDERAL GOVERNMENT WAS VIRTUALLY BROKE.

SOMEBODY CAME UP WITH A SCHEME WHICH PRESIDENT WASHINGTON APPROVED.

FEDERAL AGENTS APPROACHED EVERY LANDOWNER WITH THIS PROPOSITION...

SELL US HALF OF YOUR LAND AT £25* AN ACRE. WHEN WE ERECT PUBLIC BUILDINGS ON THAT PROPERTY, THE LAND YOU'VE KEPT WILL INCREASE IN VALUE TENFOLD

*THESE WERE MARYLAND POUNDS WORTH ABOUT $66 PER ACRE.

AND IF I REFUSE?

WE WON'T BUILD ANYTHING NEAR YOU. YOUR LAND WILL HARDLY INCREASE IN VALUE. YOU'LL SPEND THE REST OF YOUR LIFE WORKING — AS A FARMER.

OH! AH... WELL, HOW MANY ACRES DO YOU WANT?

The Settlers' Monument

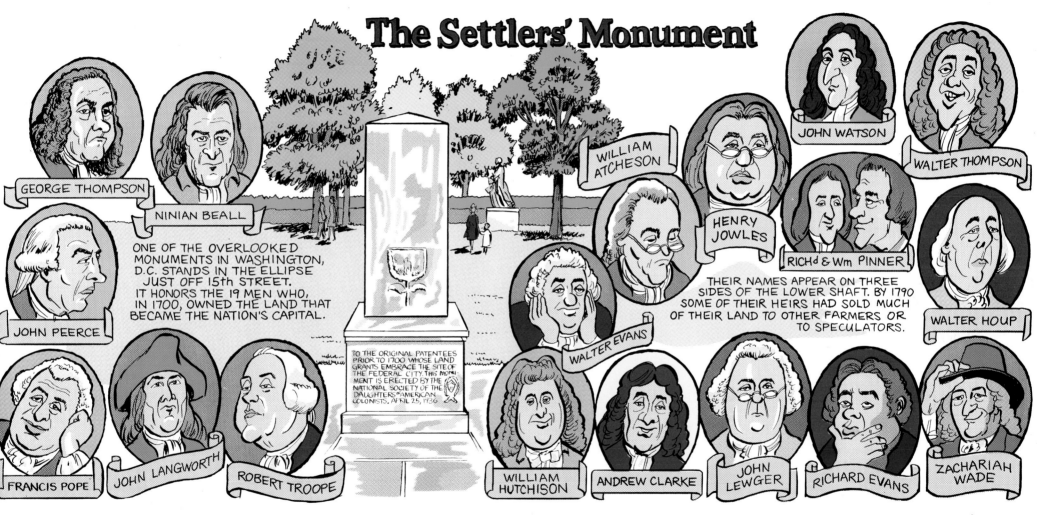

ONE OF THE OVERLOOKED MONUMENTS IN WASHINGTON, D.C. STANDS IN THE ELLIPSE JUST OFF 15th STREET. IT HONORS THE 19 MEN WHO, IN 1700, OWNED THE LAND THAT BECAME THE NATION'S CAPITAL.

TO THE ORIGINAL PATENTEES PRIOR TO 1700 WHOSE LAND GRANTS EMBRACE THE SITE OF THE FEDERAL CITY. THIS MONUMENT IS ERECTED BY THE NATIONAL SOCIETY OF THE DAUGHTERS OF AMERICAN COLONISTS. APRIL 25, 1936

THEIR NAMES APPEAR ON THREE SIDES OF THE LOWER SHAFT. BY 1790 SOME OF THEIR HEIRS HAD SOLD MUCH OF THEIR LAND TO OTHER FARMERS OR TO SPECULATORS.

GEORGE THOMPSON

NINIAN BEALL

JOHN PEERCE

FRANCIS POPE

JOHN LANGWORTH

ROBERT TROOPE

WILLIAM ATCHESON

HENRY JOWLES

JOHN WATSON

WALTER THOMPSON

RICHᵈ & Wᵐ PINNER

WALTER HOUP

WALTER EVANS

WILLIAM HUTCHISON

ANDREW CLARKE

JOHN LEWGER

RICHARD EVANS

ZACHARIAH WADE

The property of the original nineteen landowners of Washington, DC changed hands many times during the 18th century, usually within the same small circle of people.

Many of these people were related by marriage. Most of them apparently knew each other through civic service, militia service, and church activities.

19

By the time the federal government was ready to purchase property for the new capital, the most prominent landowner was David Burnes, a successful farmer and county magistrate.

Stubborn Ol' Davey Burnes

BY 1790 THE ORIGINAL 19 LANDOWNERS OF WASHINGTON, D.C. WERE DEAD AND THEIR HOLDINGS HAD BEEN BEQUEATHED OR SOLD. ONE OF THE "NEW" OWNERS WAS DAVID BURNES. WHEN THE FEDERAL GOVERNMENT OFFERED TO BUY SOME OF HIS LAND TO BUILD THE U.S. CAPITAL, BURNES BALKED.

PRESIDENT WASHINGTON APPROACHED HIM PERSONALLY.

...BUT FOR THE FEDERAL CITY RISING HERE, YOUR FARM WOULD BE WORTHLESS!

TO WHICH BURNES REPLIED,

...BUT FOR MARRYIN' THE RICH WIDOW CUSTIS, YOU TOO WOULD NOT BE WORTH MUCH!

WASHINGTON EVENTUALLY CONVINCED BURNES TO SELL. THE STUBBORN SCOTSMAN WENT ON TO BECOME VERY RICH ON THE VALUE OF HIS REMAINING FARMLAND. PART OF HIS FARM NOW LIES BETWEEN THE WHITE HOUSE AND CONSTITUTION AVENUE.

Most of the farms in the capital district were purchased by financiers and speculators. The new owners of choice lands were Samuel Blodgett, John Davidson, Daniel Carroll, William Prout, Robert Morris, and John Nicholson.

AUCTIONS & RAFFLES

After purchasing the land for the new national capital—Washington, D.C., the federal government held a series of auctions in 1791.

For sale were lots situated around land where public buildings would be erected

Some parcels were raffled—anything to pay for the construction of the federal buildings.

TODAY'S SALE
DAN. CARROLL EST.

CAPITOL

Key
Park Land
Federal Bldg
Lot For Sale

President Washington not only helped at the auctions, he purchased some lots for his own use.

Most people had no faith in the planned city. Consequently, only a few citizens made bids on the lots or bought raffle tickets. The government was stymied until Virginia gave $120,000 and Maryland donated $72,000 to get construction started.

James Gilchrist came down from Philadelphia for this auction and was the biggest buyer, spending more than $1,000 for four lots. Jacob Walsh from Boston bought five lots. Nicholas Kirby from Baltimore purchased three lots.

The Potomac Navigation Company was chartered by Maryland and Virginia in 1785 for the purpose of developing the Potomac River for commercial shipping. They employed slaves and laborers to clear rocks and debris from the river channel.

Known as the Potomac Company, its Chief Executive Officer was George Washington. Other major stockholders were prominent politicians including all the men in this story.

Washington resigned in 1789 to become president of the United States and was succeeded by Thomas Johnson.

PRESIDENT GEORGE WASHINGTON NEEDED PEOPLE TO MANAGE THE DAY TO DAY BUSINESS OF ERECTING THE NEW CAPITAL ON THE POTOMAC RIVER.

ON JANUARY 24, 1791 PRESIDENT WASHINGTON APPOINTED THE CAPITAL **COMMISSIONERS.**

STUART | JOHNSON | CARROLL

THOMAS JOHNSON HAD NOMINATED WASHINGTON FOR COMMANDER-IN-CHIEF BACK IN 1775, THEN SERVED AS GOVERNOR OF MARYLAND.

DANIEL CARROLL LIVED AT JOSEPH'S PARK, A 4,000 ACRE PLANTATION NORTHEAST OF **GEORGETOWN.** A LARGE SLAVEHOLDER, HE ALSO OWNED THOUSANDS OF ACRES IN MONTGOMERY COUNTY, MARYLAND.

THOMAS JEFFERSON, NOT AN ADVOCATE OF A STRONG FEDERAL GOVERNMENT, COMMENTED...

THEY'RE ALL BUSINESS ASSOCIATES OF MR. WASHINGTON AND READY TO DO THE PRESIDENT'S BIDDING.

DAVID STUART WAS A PLANTER AND PHYSICIAN LIVING IN **ABINGDON, VIRGINIA** NEAR MOUNT VERNON. HIS WIFE WAS MARTHA WASHINGTON'S WIDOWED DAUGHTER-IN-LAW.

DESPITE OWNING AN IRON WORKS AND A PLANTATION WITH 38 SLAVES NEAR **FREDERICK, MARYLAND,** JOHNSON'S ONLY REGRET WAS THAT HE WAS NOT WEALTHIER.

Pierre Charles L'Enfant was born on August 2, 1754 in Paris, France. He grew up in an artistic environment because his father was a "Painter in ordinary to the King." At the outbreak of the American Revolution, many well-to-do young men in Europe paid their own passage across the Atlantic to join the action. L'Enfant, age 23, was one of them. Trained in engineering and architecture, he was commissioned as a lieutenant of engineers in 1777.

The Man Who Designed Washington, D.C.

DURING THE WINTER OF 1777-78 AT VALLEY FORGE L'ENFANT SKETCHED SOME SOLDIERS INCLUDING LAFAYETTE. GENERAL WASHINGTON WAS IMPRESSED BY HIS TALENT.

TWO YEARS LATER L'ENFANT WAS WOUNDED LEADING AN ASSAULT ON SAVANNAH, GEORGIA.

CAPTURED AT CHARLESTON, SC, HE WAS RELEASED IN 1781, PROMOTED TO MAJOR, AND DISCHARGED.

AFTER THE WAR L'ENFANT BECAME A FREE-LANCE DESIGNER IN NEW YORK CITY.

HIS FIRST IMPORTANT JOB WAS TO DESIGN A PAVILION TO SEAT 6,000 PEOPLE—USED ON JULY 23, 1788 AS PART OF A CELEBRATION OF THE ADOPTION OF THE U.S. CONSTITUTION.

The winter at Valley Forge left L'Enfant with a hunger for action, so he asked for a transfer to the Southern army. He was reassigned to the light infantry under Lt. Colonel Laurens. A while later Pierre was promoted to captain.

L'Enfant's major work in New York was the remodeling of the old City Hall into the first Capitol of the U. S. Private funds had been raised but L'Enfant's habit of doing things "en grand" soon doubled the cost. The Frenchman's finished product, now called Federal Hall, won general praise for its noble appearance, but the Anti-Federalists called it the "Fool's Trap," meaning a place for politicians to congregate.

Grandiloquent Notions

PRESIDENT GEORGE WASHINGTON WAS INAUGURATED ON THE BALCONY OF THIS BUILDING ON APRIL 20, 1789.

FEDERAL HALL WAS REPLACED BY THE SUB TREASURY BUILDING ON WALL STREET. THE ONLY RELIC OF THE OLD FEDERAL BUILDING IS A PIECE OF THE WROUGHT IRON RAILING PRESERVED AT THE NEW YORK HISTORICAL SOCIETY.

RIGHT AFTER CONGRESS VOTED TO CREATE A NEW CAPITAL, L'ENFANT APPLIED FOR THE COMMISSION TO DESIGN THE NEW CITY.

...PRESIDENT WASHINGTON...

...THE PLAN SHOULD BE DRAWN ON SUCH A SCALE AS TO LEAVE ROOM FOR THE AGGRANDIZEMENT AND EMBELLISHMENT WHICH THE INCREASE OF THE WEALTH OF THE NATION WILL PERMIT IT TO PURSUE...

PRESIDENT WASHINGTON WAS AN ADMIRER OF L'ENFANT'S TALENT. A FEW YEARS EARLIER, THE FRENCHMAN DESIGNED THE INSIGNIA FOR THE SOCIETY OF THE CINCINNATI WHEN MR. WASHINGTON PRESIDED OVER THE ORGANIZATION.

I LIKE L'ENFANT'S GRANDILOQUENT NOTIONS AND SENSE OF SCALE. HE IS HIRED TO DESIGN THE NEW FEDERAL CITY.

12/11

AS SOON AS L'ENFANT RECEIVED THE ASSIGNMENT HE DEPARTED FOR GEORGETOWN, MARYLAND TO INVESTIGATE THE SITE. ALONG THE WAY HIS STAGECOACH BROKE DOWN. HE RODE A HORSE FOR A WHILE AND FINALLY WALKED THE REST OF THE WAY.

L'Enfant presented the first draft of his plan to President Washington in June, 1791. The Chief Executive did not like where the President's House was located so he had the architect move it further west to higher ground. He also ordered the number of diagonal streets to be decreased.

L'Enfant's Plan

FOR WASHINGTON, D.C. WAS COMPLETED IN AUGUST, 1791. THE FRENCH DESIGNER PRESENTED IT TO PRESIDENT WASHINGTON.

THE PRESIDENT'S HOUSE

THE EAST-WEST STREETS WILL HAVE ALPHABETICAL NAMES— C STREET, D STREET, AND SO ON. THE NORTH-SOUTH STREETS WILL BE NUMERICAL—14th STREET, 15th STREET, ETC. THE DIAGONAL AVENUES WILL BE NAMED AFTER STATES.

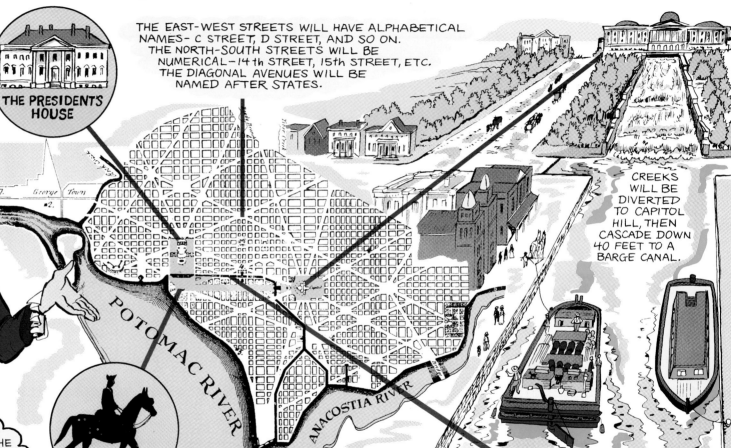

POTOMAC RIVER

ANACOSTIA RIVER

CREEKS WILL BE DIVERTED TO CAPITOL HILL, THEN CASCADE DOWN 40 FEET TO A BARGE CANAL.

MAJOR AVENUES WILL RADIATE FROM THE PRESIDENT'S HOUSE AND THE CAPITOL TO ALL PARTS OF THE CITY. ORDINARY STREETS WILL BE 90 AND 130 FEET WIDE. MAJOR AVENUES WILL BE 180 AND 400 FEET ACROSS.

EQUESTRIAN STATUE OF GEORGE WASHINGTON (NEVER ERECTED)

TIBER CREEK WAS TO BE CONVERTED INTO A CANAL. IT IS NOW CONSTITUTION AVENUE.

12/18

When Pierre L'Enfant was designing the District of Columbia he decided that the Congress House, or **Capitol**, would be situated atop **Jenkins Hill.**

A MILE AND A HALF AWAY WAS ANOTHER HILL COVERED BY AN **ORCHARD** WHERE HE PLANNED TO ERECT THE **PRESIDENT'S PALACE,** LATER CALLED THE WHITE HOUSE.

THE CAPITAL COMMISSIONERS RENTED **SLAVES** FROM NEARBY PLANTATION OWNERS TO CUT A BROAD STREET THROUGH THE FOREST CONNECTING THE TWO HILLS.

TO PLACATE THE POLITICIANS WHO CLAMORED THE LOUDEST TO KEEP PHILADELPHIA AS THE PERMANENT CAPITAL, CONGRESS NAMED THIS STREET **PENNSYLVANIA AVENUE.**

The designer of Washington was criticized for being too extravagant and unyeilding in his plans, and for being overly temperamental. For his plan to succeed, he needed all these qualities. The city had to be done on a grand scale or not at all. Actually, L'Enfant was no more tempermental and insistent than any other good architect, then or now.

THE FIRST RESPONSIBILITY OF THE DISTRICT COMMISSIONERS WAS TO OVERSEE THE CONSTRUCTION OF WASHINGTON, D.C. EVERYONE INVOLVED, INCLUDING PIERRE L'ENFANT, WAS ANSWERABLE TO THE TRIO. FROM THE OUTSET, L'ENFANT CLASHED WITH THEM.

THE STREETS ARE TOO WIDE.

THERE ARE MORE PARKS THAN NECESSARY.

REDUCE BOTH.

YOU POLITICIANS KNOW ABSOLUTELY **NOTHING** ABOUT ARCHITECTURE! **I WILL NOT** ANSWER TO YOU.

THE COMMISSIONERS ORDERED AN EARLY AUCTION OF BUILDING LOTS TO THE PUBLIC, BUT L'ENFANT REFUSED TO TURN OVER HIS PLANS SO THEY COULD CONDUCT THE SALE.

THE LOTS SHOULD BE HELD UNTIL THEY ARE WORTH MORE.

THE AUCTION WENT ON ANYWAY, BUT IT WAS A FLOP. ONLY 35 LOTS WERE SOLD FOR A TOTAL OF $8,756.

BESIDES, SPECULATORS WILL BUY UP THE BEST LOTS TO HOLD FOR HIGH PROFITS LATER.

NEED I SAY I TOLD YOU SO?

AW-W-W SHADDUP!

GO AWAY, L'ENFANT!

CAUGHT IN THE MIDDLE OF THIS SQUABBLE WAS PRESIDENT WASHINGTON WHO WAS FORCED TO ACT AS PEACEMAKER.

Immediately after L'Enfant arrived in Georgetown to plan the capital, Daniel Carroll of Duddington asked the Frenchman if he could build a house in the new city. Months passed without an answer.

TIRED OF L'ENFANT'S STALLING, MR. CARROLL FINALLY WENT AHEAD AND BUILT THE HOUSE.

CARROLL WAS A MEMBER OF THE MOST PROMINENT FAMILY IN MARYLAND AND OWNED THE MOST LAND IN WASHINGTON.

IN ADDITION, HIS UNCLE, DANIEL CARROLL, WAS A DISTRICT COMMISSIONER.

CARROLL'S HOUSE HAPPENED TO INTERFERE WITH L'ENFANT'S GRAND PLAN FOR THE CITY.

THAT IS RIGHT IN THE MIDDLE OF WHAT WILL BE NEW JERSEY AVENUE.

L'ENFANT SUMMONED HIS AIDE **ISAAC ROBERDEAU.**

MR. CARROLL IGNORES MY LETTERS. TEAR DOWN HIS HOUSE — CAREFULLY!

CARROLL ARRIVED **TOO LATE** WITH A COURT ORDER TO STOP THE DEMOLITION.

L'ENFANT EXPLAINED,

IF WE DIVERT THE STREET TO MISS YOUR HOUSE, WE WILL HAVE TO KNOCK DOWN YOUR AUNT'S MANSION.

ANXIOUS TO AVOID A LAWSUIT, THE COMMISSIONERS PROMISED MR. CARROLL,

LOOK, NEPHEW, SOMEHOW WE WILL RAISE ENOUGH FUNDS TO REIMBURSE YOUR LOSS.

PRESIDENT WASHINGTON INSTRUCTED THOMAS JEFFERSON TO DRAFT A LETTER TO THE ARCHITECT.

I STILL WANT L'ENFANT ON THE JOB, BUT **HE MUST OBEY THE COMMISSIONERS.**

Another landowner, Notley Young, had built a mansion in the general area of Constitution Avenue. At first, L'Enfant assured him that the structure was fine where it stood. Then, just as the events in this story were unfolding, the architect wrote to Mr. Young saying that his mansion would have to be torn down in about five years. Notley almost went nuts.

His complaints to the commissioners helped bring about the downfall of L'Enfant.

NO TRESPASSING

PIERRE L'ENFANT PLANNED TO TRAVEL TO PHILADELPHIA TO GET HIS PLANS FOR WASHINGTON PRINTED AND DISTRIBUTED. BEFORE LEAVING HE PUT HIS ASSISTANT, ISAAC ROBERDEAU IN CHARGE OF CONSTRUCTING THE CITY.

CONTINUE CLEARING TREES FOR THE STREETS, LEVEL THE AREA FOR THE CAPITOL, AND BUILD BARRACKS FOR 600 TO 800 WORKERS.

THEN, IN CLEAR VIOLATION OF PRESIDENT WASHINGTON'S ORDERS, L'ENFANT ADDED,

IF THE COMMISSIONERS GIVE YOU ANY ORDERS, **IGNORE THEM!**

ALL THEY'RE GOOD FOR IS **SIGNING CHECKS.**

AFTER L'ENFANT LEFT, THE COMMISSIONERS SUMMONED ROBERDEAU TO A MEETING ON JANUARY 7, 1792.

FIRE YOUR WORKMEN!

IT IS TOO COSTLY TO KEEP MEN WORKING IN THE WINTER.

ROBERDEAU'S MEN WENT ON WORKING, SO THE COMMISSIONERS ORDERED HIM TO **STAY OFF FEDERAL PROPERTY, OR ELSE.**

ISAAC KEPT HIS MEN ON THE JOB ANYWAY. WHEN THE COMMISSIONERS FOUND OUT...

THEY HAD HIM ARRESTED FOR TRESPASSING AND THROWN IN JAIL.

There were many critics of the proposed new national capital. To counteract them, L'Enfant had the *Gazette of the United States* publish his written explanation of the plan which included "...a church for all denominations for public prayer, funeral orations, etc..." In addition, each state would control a city square. None of this was true, but it put off the critics for a while.

The Final Insult

PIERRE L'ENFANT ARRIVED IN PHILADELPHIA, THE TEMPORARY CAPITAL OF THE UNITED STATES, IN LATE DECEMBER, 1791, AND MET WITH PRESIDENT WASHINGTON.

GET THE PLAN FOR THE NEW CAPITAL ENGRAVED AS SOON AS POSSIBLE.

INSTEAD, PIERRE WORKED ON A PROPOSAL TO GET A MILLION DOLLAR LOAN FROM DUTCH BANKERS TO BUILD THE CITY.

LET'S SEE...WE'LL NEED 1,070 MEN BY SPRING PLUS **$350,000** WORTH OF SUPPLIES...

IN MID FEBRUARY, 1792 PRESIDENT WASHINGTON RECEIVED MORE BAD NEWS.

SIR, IT'S BEEN SIX WEEKS AND NOTHING HAS BEEN DONE ON THE ENGRAVING OF THE CAPITAL PLANS.

MEANWHILE, WASHINGTON LEARNED THAT L'ENFANT'S AIDE, ROBERDEAU, HAD BEEN JAILED FOR DEFYING THE ORDERS OF THE COMMISSIONERS.

THE CONDUCT OF L'ENFANT AND THOSE EMPLOYED UNDER HIM ASTONISHES ME BEYOND MEANS!

THE PRESIDENT SENT HIS SECRETARY, TOBIAS LEAR, TO REMIND L'ENFANT ABOUT THE EXECUTIVE ORDER TO OBEY THE COMMISSIONERS.

I HAVE ALREADY HEARD ENOUGH OF THIS MATTER.

THEN, THE COMMISSIONERS THREATENED TO RESIGN UNLESS SOMETHING WAS DONE ABOUT L'ENFANT.

TO WASHINGTON, L'ENFANT'S RETORT WAS THE **FINAL INSULT.** HE HAD THOMAS JEFFERSON DRAFT A LETTER

February 27, 1792
Dear Mr. L'Enfant,
I am entrusted by the presid
to inform you that
your services must be
at an end.

President Washington promised Commissioner Stuart that L'Enfant *would never work in Washington again.* However, the President offered to pay the Frenchman 500 guineas. Major L'Enfant refused to take the money.

L'Enfant had several reason for not accepting cash for designing the District of Columbia. For one thing, he felt that it would would give the impression that he recognized the commissioners as his superiors. Secondly, he wanted to hold out for royalties on the sale of prints of his design. Lastly, he thought he would get a percentage of the money spent to build the city.

What Ever Happened to Pierre L'Enfant

A FEW MONTHS AFTER HE WAS FIRED AS THE ARCHITECT OF WASHINGTON, DC, PIERRE L'ENFANT WAS COMMISSIONED BY ALEXANDER HAMILTON TO DESIGN A MANUFACTURING TOWN KNOWN TODAY AS **PATERSON, NEW JERSEY.**

FORT WASHINGTON ON THE POTOMAC WAS DESTROYED DURING THE WAR OF 1812. L'ENFANT REDESIGNED IT AND HIS FINISHED PRODUCT IS NOW A NATIONAL PARK IN MARYLAND.

FOR THE REST OF HIS LIFE, PIERRE STALKED THE HALLS OF THE CAPITOL, BADGERING CONGRESS TO PAY HIM WHAT HE FELT HE WAS WORTH FOR DESIGNING WASHINGTON, DC.

CONGRESS TWICE VOTED TO SEND HIM FUNDS, BUT THE MONEY WENT DIRECTLY TO HIS CREDITORS.

HIS LAST YEARS WERE SPENT WITH THE **DIGGES** FAMILY ON THEIR ESTATE, "GREEN HILL," IN **PRINCE GEORGE'S COUNTY, MD.**

L'ENFANT DIED BROKE IN 1825 AT AGE 71. HE WAS BURIED IN DIGGES' BACK YARD.

IN 1909, AT THE URGING OF AMERICAN ARCHITECTS, PRESIDENT TAFT ORDERED L'ENFANT'S BODY EXHUMED AND BROUGHT TO WASHINGTON. IT LAY IN STATE IN THE CAPITOL ROTUNDA.

MAJOR L'ENFANT NOW LIES IN THIS TOMB IN ARLINGTON NATIONAL CEMETERY.

Another facet in the development of Washington, DC was **surveying** the land. The story of one of the key surveyors started over a century before a sextant was aimed in the new city.

England during the 17th century imposed the death penalty for over 300 types of crime. Innocent people were often convicted of crimes in order to ship them to the American colonies to work on the plantations.

The Indentured Servant Option

AROUND 1682 A YOUNG FARMHAND NAMED MOLLY WELSH WAS MILKING A COW ON AN ESTATE IN WESSEX COUNTY, ENGLAND WHEN THE BOVINE KICKED OVER A BUCKET.

UH-OH!

BOP!

HER BOSS ACCUSED HER OF STEALING THE MILK.

IN THOSE DAYS THE PENALTY FOR STEALING WAS **HANGING.**

MOLLY WAS CONVICTED, BUT SHE "CALLED FOR THE BOOK."

IF A CONVICT COULD READ, THE DEATH SENTENCE WAS LIFTED.

AH-DER... EH... UM... D-U-U-H...

GET THE ROPE!

MOST LITERATE CONVICTS WERE SENT TO THE COLONIES IN AMERICA TO WORK AS INDENTURED SERVANTS ON PLANTATIONS OWNED BY BRITISH ARISTOCRATS

MOLLY GAZED AT THE BOOK.

AND RUTH SAID, 'ENTREAT ME NOT TO LEAVE THEE OR TO RETURN FROM FOLLOWING AFTER THEE.

SO, MOLLY WELSH WAS SENT TO THE COLONY OF MARYLAND.

Notices of the arrival of these ships were posted at ports along the Chesapeake Bay. This one appeared in the *Maryland Gazette:* "Just imported from Bristol, the Ship *Rudolph*, Captain John Wever Price, 115 convicts: men, women, and lads. Among them are several tradesmen who are to be sold on board the said ship, now in Annapolis Dock. This day, tomorrow."

CONVICTED OF THEFT AND SENTENCED TO HANG IN ENGLAND, MOLLY WELSH SAVED HERSELF BY PROVING SHE COULD READ. CONSEQUENTLY SHE WAS SENT TO MARYLAND IN 1683 WITH A SHIP-LOAD OF 150 OTHER CONVICTS.

MOLLY WAS SOLD AT AN AUCTION IN ANNAPOLIS TO A TOBACCO FARMER WHOSE PLANTATION WAS NEAR PRESENT-DAY BALTIMORE.

The Seven Year Stretch

MOLLY WAS REQUIRED TO WORK FOR SEVEN YEARS AS AN INDENTURED SERVANT TO PAY FOR HER VOYAGE TO AMERICA AND HER FREEDOM.

BY 1690 MOLLY HAD EARNED HER FREEDOM. SHE RENTED AN UNDEVELOPED TRACT OF LAND ALONG THE PATAPSCO RIVER AND COOPERS CREEK. ALL BY HERSELF SHE STARTED TO TURN IT INTO A TOBACCO FARM.

33

Molly had no friends because hardly anyone lived nearby. It is possible that she sometimes received help from neighboring planters or their employees.

Molly's Plantation

FORMER INDENTURED SERVANT MOLLY WELSH SOON BECAME A SUCCESSFUL TOBACCO FARMER. BY 1692 HER PLANTATION IN MARYLAND WAS TOO MUCH TO HANDLE BY HERSELF.

ALTHOUGH SHE HATED SLAVERY, SLAVES WERE THE ONLY FARM HANDS AVAILABLE. SHE AGONIZED OVER MAKING A DECISION FOR MONTHS. FINALLY...

SHE PURCHASED TWO SLAVES. ONE WAS HARD-WORKING, BUT THE OTHER...

ME.. I... NO.. WORK HARD. IN AFRICA... I AM SON OF CHIEFTAN. CALL ME **BANNEKY!**

IN 1696 MOLLY GAVE BOTH SLAVES THEIR **FREEDOM.**

MEANWHILE BANNEKY AND MOLLY HAD FALLEN IN LOVE.

DESPITE THE SOCIAL AND LEGAL OBSTACLES AT THAT TIME, THEY GOT MARRIED IN 1699. EVENTUALLY THE BANNEKY FAMILY HAD FOUR DAUGHTERS.

34

A law enacted in Maryland in 1684 stated that "...a white woman who married a Negro or bore his child forfeited her freedom and became a servant *to the use of the Minister of the Poor of the same Parish."* Molly was either unaware of that law or she figured her farm in the boondocks was too remote to attract the attention of the authorities.

A TOBACCO PLANTER IN MARYLAND, MOLLY WELSH MARRIED HER FREED SLAVE, **BANNEKY**, IN 1699. HE WAS KILLED BY A YELLOW FEVER EPIDEMIC IN THE EARLY 1700's.

BANNEKY AND MOLLY HAD FOUR DAUGHTERS. MARY, THE OLDEST, MARRIED AN EX-SLAVE NAMED ROBERT IN 1730. THE COUPLE USED THE SURNAME **BANNEKY** WHICH WAS GRADUALLY CHANGED TO

BANNEKER.

THEY LIVED AND WORKED ON MOLLY'S PLANTATION.

THEIR FIRST CHILD, BENJAMIN, WAS BORN ON NOV. 9, 1731.

REMEMBERING HOW THE ABILITY TO READ SAVED HER LIFE, MOLLY TAUGHT HER GRANDSON TO READ BEFORE HE COULD WALK.

BEN BANNEKER WOULD GO ON TO HAVE AN IMPORTANT ROLE IN THE DEVELOPMENT OF WASHINGTON, D.C.

BENJAMIN BANNEKER WAS ONE OF SEVERAL CHILDREN BORN TO FREE AFRICANS IN MARYLAND. WHEN HE WAS SIX, IN 1737, HIS PARENTS PURCHASED A FARM NEAR ELK RIDGE LANDING ALONG THE PATAPSCO RIVER.

THE WOODEN CLOCK

WHEN BEN WAS 28, IN 1759, HIS FATHER DIED AND HE INHERITED THE PLANTATION. HE WORKED AS A TOBACCO FARMER FOR THE REST OF HIS LIFE, BUT HIS PASSION WAS THE STUDY OF MATHEMATICS AND SCIENCE.

ONE DAY A FRIEND, JOSEF LEVI, GAVE HIM A WATCH. BEN DECIDED TO MAKE HIS OWN CLOCK. FIRST, HE DISASSEMBLED THE WATCH, THEN DREW EACH OF THE PARTS.

UNABLE TO AFFORD GOLD OR SILVER, BEN MADE THE CLOCK OUT OF WOOD. IT TOOK HIM OVER TWO YEARS TO HAND CARVE EVERY PIECE AND ASSEMBLE THE TIMEPIECE.

COMPLETED IN 1768, IT WAS THE **FIRST CLOCK BUILT ENTIRELY IN AMERICA.** PEOPLE CAME FROM MILES AROUND TO SEE IT, MAKING MR. BANNEKER A LOCAL CELEBRITY.

THE OBSERVATORY

BENJAMIN BANNEKER NEVER MARRIED. HIS TIME WAS DIVIDED BETWEEN WORKING ON HIS TOBACCO PLANTATION AND STUDYING MATHEMATICS AND SCIENCE

AROUND 1760 HE BUILT A "WORK CABIN" ON A HILL NEAR PRESENT-DAY **ELLICOTT CITY, MARYLAND**.

THE CABIN WAS ACTUALLY AN OBSERVATORY WHERE EVERY NIGHT FOR OVER 30 YEARS MR. BANNEKER WORKED ON ASTRONOMY.

HE ACCURATELY PREDICTED NOT ONLY THE LOCATION OF PLANETS AND STARS, BUT THE EXACT DATES OF ECLIPSES.

BEN WAS 60 YEARS OLD AND RETIRED FROM FARMING WHEN, IN 1791, HE WAS VISITED BY MAJOR ANDREW ELLICOTT.

MY COUSIN GEORGE, YOUR NEIGHBOR, SAID YOU COULD HELP ME. I NEED AN **ASTRONOMER** TO ASSIST ME IN **SURVEYING** THE NEW CAPITAL CITY ON THE POTOMAC. **WILL YOU TAKE THE JOB?**

The Ellicott family originally settled in Bucks County, Pennsylvania. In December, 1766, Joseph inherited his great-grandfather's estate in Devonshire, England, so he went there to collect his money, 1,500 pounds sterling.

While in London, he learned clock making from a relative. On returning to America, he taught the trade to his son, Andrew. Joseph Ellicott also used his inheritance to buy property in Maryland and start several businesses.

AROUND 1770 JOE ELLICOTT FOUNDED **ELLICOTT'S UPPER MILLS,** AN INDUSTRIAL TOWN IN MARYLAND.

JOSEPH AND JUDITH ELLICOTT HAD NINE CHILDREN. THEIR OLDEST, **ANDREW,** WORKED IN ONE OF THE FAMILY'S ENTERPRISES— **MAKING CLOCKS.**

AT THE OUTBREAK OF THE REVOLUTIONARY WAR IN 1775, ANDREW, THEN 21 YEARS OLD, JOINED THE MARYLAND MILITIA. HE ATTAINED THE RANK OF MAJOR AND, THEREAFTER, REFERRED TO HIMSELF AS **MAJOR ELLICOTT.**

ANDREW RETURNED TO THE CLOCK BUSINESS IN 1780. HE DEVELOPED AN INTEREST IN **SURVEYING** AND STARTED TO CREATE INSTRUMENTS FOR USE IN THE FIELD.

THEN, IN 1784, HE WAS APPOINTED TO A COMMISSION WHICH INCLUDED DAVID RITTENHOUSE OF NORRISTOWN, PENNSYLVANIA. THEIR JOB WAS TO SURVEY THE BOUNDARY BETWEEN WESTERN PENNSYLVANIA AND VIRGINIA—NOW WEST VIRGINIA.

OHIO
PENNSYLVANIA
OHIO RIVER
ALLEGHENY RIVER
PITTSBURGH
MONONGAHELA
VIRGINIA
MD

SPECIAL FOOTNOTE— RITTENHOUSE, ALSO A CLOCK MAKER, WENT ON TO BECOME THE **FIRST DIRECTOR OF THE U.S. MINT.**

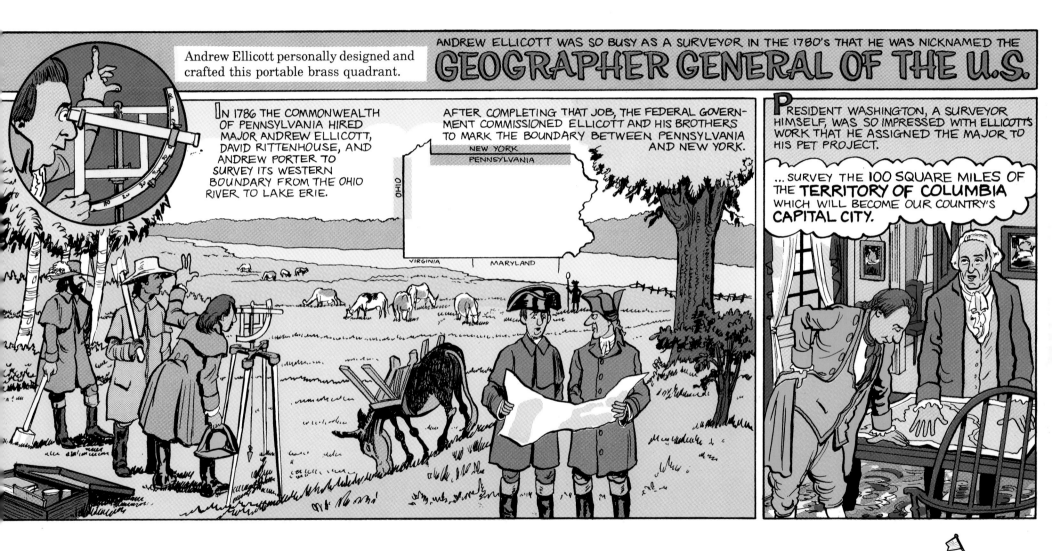

Andrew Ellicott personally designed and crafted this portable brass quadrant.

IN 1786 THE COMMONWEALTH OF PENNSYLVANIA HIRED MAJOR ANDREW ELLICOTT, DAVID RITTENHOUSE, AND ANDREW PORTER TO SURVEY ITS WESTERN BOUNDARY FROM THE OHIO RIVER TO LAKE ERIE.

AFTER COMPLETING THAT JOB, THE FEDERAL GOVERNMENT COMMISSIONED ELLICOTT AND HIS BROTHERS TO MARK THE BOUNDARY BETWEEN PENNSYLVANIA AND NEW YORK.

NEW YORK
PENNSYLVANIA
OHIO
VIRGINIA   MARYLAND

PRESIDENT WASHINGTON, A SURVEYOR HIMSELF, WAS SO IMPRESSED WITH ELLICOTT'S WORK THAT HE ASSIGNED THE MAJOR TO HIS PET PROJECT.

...SURVEY THE 100 SQUARE MILES OF THE **TERRITORY OF COLUMBIA** WHICH WILL BECOME OUR COUNTRY'S **CAPITAL CITY.**

All did not go smoothly for the members of the survey team. Several died from illness.

One man was killed by a falling tree.

ANDREW ELLICOTT'S SURVEY PARTY ARRIVED IN ALEXANDRIA, VIRGINIA IN EARLY FEBRUARY, 1791. THEY SET UP CAMP ON UPPER ROCK CREEK.

FIRST, BENJAMIN **BANNEKER**, THE GROUP'S ASTRONOMER, HAD TO FIND THE EXACT STARTING POINT ON THE GROUND. TO DO THIS...

HE OBSERVED AND PLOTTED ABOUT SIX STARS AS THEY CROSSED HIS SPOT AT A PARTICULAR TIME OF NIGHT.

THE SURVEYORS STARTED AT JONES POINT AT HUNTING CREEK IN ALEXANDRIA, THEN CROSSED THE POTOMAC TO MARYLAND. ELLICOTT'S TOPOGRAPHICAL ASSISTANT, ISAAC ROBERDEAU, TOOK CHARGE OF THE FIELD TEAM.

CHOP! WHAP!
CHOP! CHOP!
CHOP!

THE FIELD TEAM CONSISTED OF CHAIN MEN, AXMEN, AND LABORERS.

ROBERDEAU'S FIELD TEAM CLEARED A 40-FOOT WIDE SWATH AFTER THE SURVEYORS MADE SIGHTINGS. EACH OF THE 4 SWATHS WAS TEN MILES LONG AND DEFINED THE BOUNDARY OF THE DISTRICT OF COLUMBIA.

While the survey of the preliminary lines was in progress, President Washington decided to check on things. Arriving on the morning of March 28, 1791, he met with the three commissioners, then rode out to the survey camp. The President and his entourage had dinner at Suter's Tavern. Afterwards, Mr. Washington looked at Ellicott's drawings and expressed his satisfaction.

The Cornerstone of D.C.

BENJAMIN BANNEKER AND ANDREW ELLICOTT LOCATED THE STARTING POINT FOR THE BOUNDARY OF THE FEDERAL DISTRICT AT **JONES POINT** IN ALEXANDRIA, VIRGINIA IN EARLY APRIL, 1791.

IMMEDIATELY, MASON LODGE NUMBER 22 OF ALEXANDRIA (GEORGE WASHINGTON WAS A MEMBER) PLANNED AN ELABORATE CEREMONY TO LAY THE CORNERSTONE.

ON APRIL 15, 1791 DR. ELISH DICK, WORSHIPFUL MASTER OF LODGE 22, LED A PROCESSION OF MASONS, DIGNITARIES, AND "STRANGERS" TO JONES POINT.

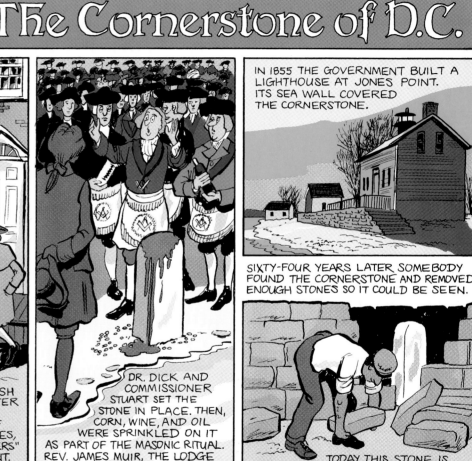

DR. DICK AND COMMISSIONER STUART SET THE STONE IN PLACE. THEN, CORN, WINE, AND OIL WERE SPRINKLED ON IT AS PART OF THE MASONIC RITUAL. REV. JAMES MUIR, THE LODGE CHAPLAIN, GAVE A SPEECH.

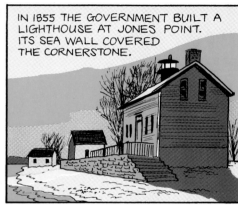

IN 1855 THE GOVERNMENT BUILT A LIGHTHOUSE AT JONES POINT. ITS SEA WALL COVERED THE CORNERSTONE.

SIXTY-FOUR YEARS LATER SOMEBODY FOUND THE CORNERSTONE AND REMOVED ENOUGH STONES SO IT COULD BE SEEN.

TODAY THIS STONE IS SURROUNDED BY AN IRON GRATE.

George Ellicott's daughter later wrote, "Banneker's deportment throughout the whole of this engagement was such as to secure for him the admiration and the respect of the Commissioners and their staff. His striking superiority over all men of his race whom they had met, led them to disregard all prejudice of caste, and converse freely with him, and enjoy the clearness and originality of his remarks."

ANDREW ELLICOTT'S SURVEY CREW CONTINUED TO LAY OUT THE BOUNDARY OF WASHINGTON, D.C. IN THE SPRING OF 1791.

THE STRENUOUS PACE OF HIKING UP HILLS AND TRUDGING THROUGH THICK BRUSH FINALLY GOT TO THE TEAM'S 60 YEAR-OLD ASTRONOMER, BEN BANNEKER.

IN LATE APRIL, 1791 BANNEKER CALLED IT QUITS AND HEADED HOME TO HIS FARM IN HOWARD COUNTY, MARYLAND.

Ben Banneker's Almanac

BACK HOME, BANNEKER WROTE AN ALMANAC. IT WAS A COMPENDIUM OF MATHEMATICS, ASTRONOMY, ESSAYS, PROVERBS, AND JOKES.

THOMAS JEFFERSON READ PART OF BANNEKER'S MANUSCRIPT AND RECOMMENDED IT TO A PUBLISHER

BANNEKER'S ALMANAC WAS PUBLISHED ANNUALLY FROM 1792 TO 1802, MAKING BEN FAMOUS THROUGHOUT THE UNITED STATES AND EUROPE.

MEANWHILE, ELLICOTT HAD COMPLETED THE SURVEY OF THE DISTRICT OF COLUMBIA'S BOUNDARY EARLY IN 1793.

JURISDICTION OF THE UNITED STATES Miles 7

MR. BANNEKER DIED ON OCTOBER 25, 1806 AT THE AGE OF 75.

Meanwhile, Ellicott needed copies of L'Enfant's plans to complete his survey but found that the French architect neglected getting the plans engraved. Andrew promptly informed Jefferson and the President. This contributed to L'Enfant's firing. Afterwards, L'Enfant refused to turn his plans and notes over to the government. A popular myth asserts that Benjamin Banneker had seen and memorized the design. So, when the plans were needed, he simple redrew them from memory. There is no concrete evidence to support that claim.

Jefferson and President Washington trusted Ellicott and his brothers to lay out the city without L'Enfant's assistance. Andrew did not hesitate to suggest some changes to L'Enfant's original design.

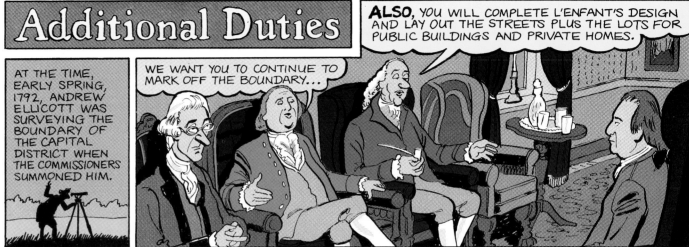

Additional Duties

AT THE TIME, EARLY SPRING, 1792, ANDREW ELLICOTT WAS SURVEYING THE BOUNDARY OF THE CAPITAL DISTRICT WHEN THE COMMISSIONERS SUMMONED HIM.

WE WANT YOU TO CONTINUE TO MARK OFF THE BOUNDARY...

ALSO, YOU WILL COMPLETE L'ENFANT'S DESIGN AND LAY OUT THE STREETS PLUS THE LOTS FOR PUBLIC BUILDINGS AND PRIVATE HOMES.

FEW WEEKS LATER...

WHAT'S TAKING YOU SO LONG?

AREN'T YOU DONE YET?

WE NEED THE LOTS SURVEYED IN A HURRY SO WE CAN SELL THEM.

I REFUSE TO HURRY. TAKING SHORT CUTS WILL ONLY LEAD TO PROBLEMS LATER ON.

ELLICOTT FOUND HIMSELF WORKING 18 HOUR DAYS TO SATISFY HIS BOSSES.

I HAVE BEEN SO BUSY THAT I SCARCELY HAVE TIME TO EITHER SHAVE OR COMB MY HEAD.

Many of Ellicott's alterations were approved but, since each step of L'Enfant's design was not documented, it is difficult to determine exactly what changes Ellicott had made.

Ellicott's reaction to the commissioners pressuring him to hurry was to withdraw into a shell. On December 14, 1792 he wrote to his wife, "I begin to dislike the whole place and have become too ill natured to associate with beings except my four assistants...I eat alone in the office, to which I confine myself as closely as a bear to his den in the winter."

The Mystery of the Sabotaged Plans

IN DECEMBER, 1792, SOMEONE WROTE A LETTER TO THE *MARYLAND JOURNAL*, PRINTED IN BALTIMORE.

ANDREW ELLICOTT'S SURVEY OF THE DISTRICT OF COLUMBIA IS FULL OF **MISTAKES!**

MEANWHILE JAMES DERMOTT, A MEMBER OF ELLICOTT'S TEAM, HAD BRAGGED...

I SHALL SOON HAVE ELLICOTT'S JOB!

ELLICOTT CHECKED THE PLANS AND FOUND PLENTY OF MISTAKES.

DERMOTT CHANGED MY CALCULATIONS. THAT'S HIS HANDWRITING!

HE WENT TO THE DISTRICT COMMISSIONERS.

...ALSO, DERMOTT **STOLE** SOME OF THE PLANS!

GIVE US YOUR EXPLANATION IN WRITING BY TOMORROW. TILL THEN, YOU ARE AT FAULT.

ELLICOTT WENT BACK TO WORK. **SEVERAL DAYS PASSED**

I'M TOO BUSY TO WRITE AN EXPLANATION

IN FEBRUARY, 1793...

WE NEVER RECEIVED YOUR WRITTEN EXPLANATION.

MR. DERMOTT FOUND THE MISSING PLANS WITH YOUR ERRORS.

WHICH MEANS YOU'RE FIRED!

BEN STODDERT, A PROMINENT MERCHANT FROM GEORGETOWN, WENT TO PRESIDENT WASHINGTON ON ELLICOTT'S BEHALF.

OKAY, I'LL ORDER THE COMMISSIONERS TO REINSTATE ELLICOTT.

ELLICOTT WAS REHIRED, BUT...

THEY DID NOT FIRE THAT THIEF AND DRUNKARD, DERMOTT.

FOR THE NEXT FIVE YEARS, EVERY SQUARE BLOCK OF WASHINGTON HAD TO BE RESURVEYED BECAUSE SOMEBODY KEPT MOVING THE STAKES AND "DOCTORING" THE PLANS.

PLOP!

Late in 1792, James Dermott had "declared that he had put the affairs of the city (Washington) into such a train, that they should never be set right again..."

ANDREW ELLICOTT WAS HAVING TROUBLE MEASURING AND MARKING OFF THE STREETS AND BUILDING LOTS OF WASHINGTON, D.C. IN THE SPRING OF 1793.

YOUR FIGURES ARE OFF!

ONE OF MY SURVEYORS, JAMES DERMOTT, HAS BEEN SNEAKING INTO MY OFFICE AND MESSING UP THE PLANS.

WE LIKE DERMOTT. YOU'RE IN CHARGE SO IT'S YOUR FAULT.

THAT'S IT. I QUIT!

AFTER ELLICOTT LEFT, HIS BROTHER, BENJAMIN, AND FRIEND, ISAAC BRIGGS, TOOK OVER HIS DUTIES.

DERMOTT ALSO REMAINED ON THE TEAM AND CONTINUED TO FOUL UP THE WORKS. BRIGGS FINALLY BLEW HIS TOP...

IMBECILE! YOU STAKED OUT THE *CANAL IN THE WRONG PLACE!

SO?

* NOW CONSTITUTION AVENUE

BRIGGS COMPLAINED TO DISTRICT COMMISSIONER THOMAS JOHNSON.

STOP PICKING ON DERMOTT AND FIX YOUR MISTAKES.

EITHER DERMOTT GOES OR I GO!

THEN, BY GOD, MR. BRIGGS, WE WISH TO HAVE NOTHING MORE TO DO WITH YOU.

BRIGGS WAS HISTORY AND SOON AFTERWARDS BEN ELLICOTT LEFT. AS HE PREDICTED, DERMOTT GOT ANDREW ELLICOTT'S JOB. NOW THE LAND SPECULATORS HAD TO DEAL WITH HIM.

HERE'S MY LAND.

ACTUALLY, IT'S YOURS AND THE MIDDLE OF P STREET.

One of the slickest salesmen in the country during the 1790's, James Greenleaf convinced two of America's most important financiers, Robert Morris and John Nicholson, that Washington was the Promised Land where millions could be made in real estate. Morris and Nicholson, both from Philadelphia, bought into his get-rich-quick scheme.

THE SPECULATORS

A PARTNERSHIP CONSISTING OF *(FROM LEFT)*:JOHN NICHOLSON, ROBERT MORRIS, AND JAMES GREENLEAF WAS ORGANIZED IN 1793 TO PURCHASE A VAST ACREAGE OF LAND IN WASHINGTON, D.C.
A GOOFED-UP CITY PLAN PREVENTED THEM FROM DEVELOPING THEIR HOLDINGS.

IN 1795 NICHOLSON WAS APPROACHED BY JAMES DERMOTT, THE DISTRICT'S CHIEF SURVEYOR.

I CAN FACILITATE AN ACCURATE SURVEY IF YOU GIVE ME TWO BUILDING LOTS.

TWO YEARS LATER...

I NEED MORE GREASING. *

＊A BRIBE

DERMOTT IS THE **WORST SCOUNDREL** I EVER KNEW.

NICHOLSON HIRED HIS OWN SURVEYORS - NICHOLAS KING AND HIS FATHER, ROBERT.

SOON NICHOLAS KING TRACED MANY OF THE MISTAKES IN THE CITY'S SURVEY TO DERMOTT. NICHOLSON BROUGHT THIS EVIDENCE TO THE DISTRICT COMMISSIONERS.

AH...WE...ER... UM...DUH...

I SUGGEST YOU MAKE SOME CHANGES.

LATE IN 1797 DERMOTT WAS "DISMISSED FOR MISCONDUCT."

NICHOLAS **KING** BECAME THE DISTRICT'S SURVEYOR AND FINALLY STRAIGHTENED OUT THE PLAN.

BY 1799 THE DEVELOPMENT OF WASHINGTON BY GREENLEAF, NICHOLSON, AND MORRIS WAS A FLOP. ALL THREE WENT BROKE.

About a year after leaving Washington, Andrew Ellicott was commissioned by Governor Thomas Mifflin of Pennsylvania to lay out the city of **Erie.** *Shown in the background of this scene is Presque Isle.*

After completing the Erie job, Ellicott spent the next two years plotting a road from there southeast to Reading, PA. Today this road roughly follows U.S. Route 322.

ELLICOTT'S CAREER

IN JUNE, 1795 HE AND GENERAL WILLIAM IRVINE STARTED THE JOB AT WHAT IS NOW PARADE AND FRONT STREETS IN ERIE.

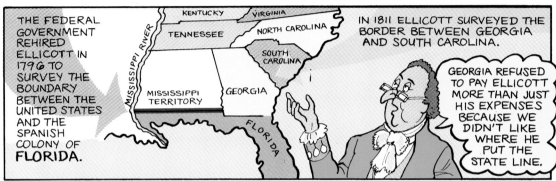

THE FEDERAL GOVERNMENT REHIRED ELLICOTT IN 1796 TO SURVEY THE BOUNDARY BETWEEN THE UNITED STATES AND THE SPANISH COLONY OF **FLORIDA.**

IN 1811 ELLICOTT SURVEYED THE BORDER BETWEEN GEORGIA AND SOUTH CAROLINA.

GEORGIA REFUSED TO PAY ELLICOTT MORE THAN JUST HIS EXPENSES BECAUSE WE DIDN'T LIKE WHERE HE PUT THE STATE LINE.

DURING THE EARLY 1800'S, ELLICOTT WORKED FOR THE PENNSYLVANIA LAND OFFICE AND LIVED AT 123 N. PRINCE ST, LANCASTER, PA. HIS HOUSE, SHOWN HERE, IS NOW ON THE NATIONAL REGISTER OF HISTORIC PLACES.

HE WENT TO THE U.S. MILITARY ACADEMY IN 1813 TO TEACH MATHEMATICS.

MR. ELLICOTT DIED AT WEST POINT ON AUGUST 28, 1820.

Section Three

Under Construction

Goofed-up planning, a shortage of skilled labor, conflicting egos, and constant bickering delay construction of the most important structures in the new Federal City: the White House and the Capitol.

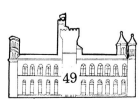

Pierre L'Enfant was originally contracted to not only lay out the city of Washington, but to design every building in it as well. However, he was constantly locking heads with the commissioners over everything from changes in the design to the schedule of the construction workers.

Finally, President Washington sided with the commissioners and fired L'Enfant. Now the commissioners had to find a way to get the buildings designed.

THE DESIGN AND CONSTRUCTION OF THE FEDERAL CITY, AS WASHINGTON, D.C. WAS FIRST CALLED, WAS IN THE HANDS OF THREE COMMISSIONERS: THOMAS JOHNSON, DAVID STUART, AND DANIEL CARROLL. EARLY IN 1792 THEY ANNOUNCED A COMPETITION FOR THE DESIGN OF THE "PRESIDENT'S HOUSE."

JAMES DIAMOND OF SOMERSET COUNTY, MARYLAND TOPPED OFF HIS DESIGN WITH A GIANT ROOSTER.

A CARPENTER NAMED PHILIP HART USED WHIMSICAL FIGURES IN HIS PLAN.

THIS DESIGN WAS SUBMITTED BY ABRAHAM FAWS WHO TURNED OUT TO BE THOMAS JEFFERSON.

I DID NOT WANT MY REAL NAME TO INFLUENCE THEIR DECISION, NOR DID I THINK I'D WIN.

HE LOST.

51

When he submitted his design for the Presidential Mansion in 1792, James Hoban had been living for the past ten years in Charleston, South Carolina, and had designed the state capitol in Columbia.

After moving to Washington, he designed Blodgett's Hotel and became politically active as a member of City Council from 1820 until his death in 1831.

JAMES HOBAN, AN IRISH ARCHITECT LIVING IN CHARLESTON, SOUTH CAROLINA, WON THE COMPETITION TO DESIGN THE PRESIDENT'S HOUSE.

IN JULY, 1792 THE DISTRICT COMMISSIONERS AWARDED HOBAN A GOLD **MEDAL** WORTH TEN GUINEAS — ABOUT **$500.**

IN ADDITION, YOU HAVE A CONTRACT FOR $1,500 A YEAR TO SUPERVISE THE CONSTRUCTION OF THE PRESIDENT'S MANSION.

HOWEVER, THERE IS A PROBLEM...

YOUR DESIGN IS TOO SMALL TO FILL ALL THE SPACE ALLOTTED IN L'ENFANT'S PLAN.

I'LL ENLARGE THE MANSION AND SURROUND IT WITH LARGE GARDENS.

ONE MAJOR QUESTION REMAINED TO BE RESOLVED...

WE'LL LET MR. WASHINGTON DECIDE EXACTLY WHERE TO PLACE THE PRESIDENT'S HOUSE.

The nation's first Presidential Mansion stood at 3 Cherry Street, in New York City. President and Mrs. Washington lived here from 1789 to 1790 when the capital was moved to Philadelphia. There they resided at 190 High Street in a house owned by Robert Morris.

ON AUGUST 2, 1792 PRESIDENT WASHINGTON RODE DOWN FROM MOUNT VERNON TO SELECT THE EXACT SPOT TO BUILD THE PRESIDENT'S HOUSE IN THE NEW FEDERAL CITY. HE CIRCLED THE AREA, CALCULATED, AND RECALCULATED. THEN, HE MADE HIS DECISION.

SITING THE WHITE HOUSE

THE FRONT DOOR ON THE NORTH WALL WILL BE HERE—PRECISELY WHERE MAJOR L'ENFANT MEANT THE FRONT DOOR TO BE ON HIS CITY PLAN.

BUT SIR, THE VIEW OF THE CAPITOL WILL BE OBSTRUCTED FROM THIS SPOT.

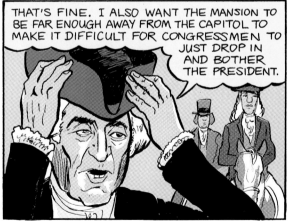

THAT'S FINE. I ALSO WANT THE MANSION TO BE FAR ENOUGH AWAY FROM THE CAPITOL TO MAKE IT DIFFICULT FOR CONGRESSMEN TO JUST DROP IN AND BOTHER THE PRESIDENT.

There was no formal ground breaking.

Some time in late August, 1792 James Hoban and a team of laborers started the foundation of the President's House. At last, the first building in the new capital city was under construction.

The Digging and the Dedication

A THICK, LEVEL BED OF RUBBLE WAS PLACED ON THE CLAY FLOOR, AND ON THAT THE ROUGH FOUNDATION STONES WERE LAID. NEXT, RECTANGULAR CUT-STONE BLOCKS WERE USED TO ERECT THE BASEMENT WALLS.

PRESIDENT WASHINGTON WAS BUSY IN PHILADELPHIA, THE TEMPORARY CAPITAL, AND COULD NOT TRAVEL TO THE POTOMAC FOR A SPECIAL CEREMONY.

ON OCTOBER 13, 1792 A PARADE OF FREEMASONS AND CITIZENS LEFT THE FOUNTAIN INN, GEORGETOWN, AND HEADED FOR THE PRESIDENT'S HOUSE.

THERE THE GRAND MASTER MADE A SPEECH, THEN PRESSED A BRASS PLATE INTO THE MORTAR ATOP THE CORNERSTONE.

IT'S INSCRIBED, "THIS FIRST STONE OF THE PRESIDENT'S HOUSE WAS LAID ON THE 13th DAY OF OCTOBER, 1792, AND IN THE 17th YEAR OF THE INDEPENDENCE OF THE UNITED STATES OF AMERICA..."

SINCE THE CORNERSTONE HAD NO SPECIAL MARKING, NOBODY CAN FIND IT TODAY.

The President's residence was officially known by three different names:

The President's House - 1800 to 1814
The Executive Mansion - 1814 to 1901
The White House - 1901 to present time.

How the White House Got Its Name

THERE ARE SEVERAL VERSIONS OF HOW THE MANSION AT 1600 PENNSYLVANIA AVE. CAME TO BE CALLED THE WHITE HOUSE.

ONE HISTORIAN CLAIMS PRESIDENT GEORGE WASHINGTON NAMED IT AFTER THE WHITE HOUSE WHERE HIS WIFE, MARTHA CUSTIS, WAS LIVING WHEN HE PROPOSED TO HER.

ANOTHER VERSION— THE BRITISH BURNED THE PRESIDENTIAL MANSION IN 1814. LATER, THE BLACKENED STONE WALLS WERE RE-PAINTED WHITE, SO FOLKS BEGAN CALLING IT THE WHITE HOUSE.

FROM THE ADMINIS-TRATION OF JAMES MONROE IN THE 1820'S UNTIL THE BEGINNING OF TEDDY ROOSEVELT'S, ITS OFFICIAL DESIGNATION WAS **THE EXECUTIVE MANSION.**

FINALLY, IN 1901, PRESIDENT TEDDY ROOSEVELT CHANGED THE OFFICIAL NAME TO THE WHITE HOUSE ON ALL PRESIDENTIAL DOCUMENTS.

The roads to Washington were quite busy in 1800 as stage-coaches, wagons, horses, and private buggies brought government workers and their families to the new capital. Joining the parade was the First Lady.

Which Way To Washington?

IN THE FALL OF 1800, **ABIGAIL ADAMS** LEFT MASSACHUSETTS TO JOIN HER HUSBAND, JOHN, AT THE RECENTLY BUILT PRESIDENTIAL MANSION IN THE NATION'S NEW CAPITAL, **WASHINGTON, D.C.**

AFTER LEAVING BALTIMORE ON NOV. 15th, HER ENTOURAGE MADE A WRONG TURN AND GOT LOST IN THE WOODS OF ANNE ARUNDEL COUNTY, MARYLAND.

FINALLY SHE ORDERED HER DRIVER TO ASK FOR DIRECTIONS. BY NOW THEY WERE HOURS BEHIND SCHEDULE.

EMBARRASSED AT BEING LATE, SHE DECIDED NOT TO STOP AT **MONTPELIER MANSION IN LAUREL, MD** WHERE SHE HAD PLANNED TO STAY OVERNIGHT.

STOP!

TOM SNOWDEN, OWNER OF MONTPELIER, HAD BEEN WAITING FOR MRS. ADAMS. HE CHASED AFTER HER CARRIAGE AND CONVINCED THE GROUP TO STAY AT HIS PLACE.

THE FIRST LADY ARRIVED IN WASHINGTON THE NEXT DAY ONLY TO FIND THE PRESIDENTIAL MANSION STILL UNDER CONSTRUCTION.

I SHOULD HAVE STAYED IN MASSACHUSETTS.

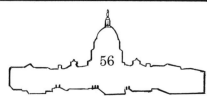

President John Adams had arrived in Washington on June 3, 1800 and was greeted by a bevy of big-shots on horseback who escorted him to his residence at Tunnicliff's Hotel, an early saloon and political hang-out. The President lived here four months until the First Lady came to town. Located on the southwest corner of 9th Street and Pennsylvania Avenue SE, Tunnicliff's was demolished in 1932 to make way for a gas station.

Welcome to the White House

THE PRESIDENTIAL MANSION, OR WHITE HOUSE, AS WE KNOW IT TODAY, WAS NOT QUITE FINISHED WHEN PRESIDENT JOHN ADAMS AND HIS WIFE, ABIGAIL, MOVED IN ON NOVEMBER 16, 1800.

WORKMEN WERE STILL LIVING IN LEAN-TO'S AGAINST THE SIDES OF THE MANSION.

INSIDE, THE STAIRS WERE NOT INSTALLED, THE WALLS WERE NOT YET PLASTERED, AND OVER A DOZEN FIRES HAD TO BE KEPT BURNING TO FIGHT THE DAMPNESS.

THE SHIP CARRYING ABIGAIL'S LUGGAGE WAS LATE, BUT WHEN IT FINALLY ARRIVED, MOST OF HER THINGS WERE EITHER **MISSING** OR **BROKEN**, INCLUDING HALF OF THE TEA CHINA.

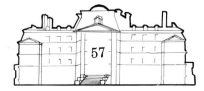

The grandest receptions ever held at the White House were those on New Year's Day. A day or two before the event, the public rooms of the mansion were closed and put into the hands of the White House decorators who raided the botanical gardens to create elaborate floral displays. The annual reception was a dress parade for the "entire official contingent," which means a power-brokers' extravaganza. The tradition was started back in 1801 by President John Adams.

The First New Year's at the White House

PRESIDENT JOHN ADAMS AND HIS WIFE, ABIGAIL HAD ONLY A BRIEF STAY IN THE WHITE HOUSE, BUT DURING THOSE FEW MONTHS, THEY TRIED TO ESTABLISH THE PROPER SOCIAL TONE FOR THE PRESIDENT'S HOME.

JOHN AND ABIGAIL HOSTED THE FIRST NEW YEAR'S RECEPTION IN THE WHITE HOUSE IN 1801. SINCE THE BUILDING WAS STILL UNDER CONSTRUCTION, THE PARTY TOOK PLACE IN THE OVAL ROOM ON THE SECOND FLOOR. THE NEW MARINE CORPS BAND PROVIDED THE ENTERTAINMENT.

MEANWHILE, THE ADAMS' LAUNDRY WAS DRYING IN THE EAST ROOM DOWNSTAIRS.

popular myth is that Washington, DC had been a swamp. Actually, the city was laid out on three terraces which rose from three streams to an elevation of one hundred feet at what became Florida Avenue.

FOR CENTURIES THE HILL HAD BEEN USED AS A CAMPSITE BY INDIANS, MOST LIKELY THE POTOWOMECKS, NATOTCHTANKS, AND MOYAONES.

"...A PEDESTAL WAITING FOR A MONUMENT."

IN THE 18th CENTURY A MAN NAMED JENKINS LEASED SOME LAND IN WHAT IS NOW WASHINGTON, D.C. AND STARTED TO FARM IT. THE OLD CAMPSITE NEARBY BECAME KNOWN AS **JENKINS HEIGHTS.**

ONE MORNING IN JUNE, 1791, PIERRE L'ENFANT, A FRENCH-BORN ENGINEER, WAS INSPECTING THE TERRAIN THAT WAS SELECTED FOR THE CITY HE WAS DESIGNING — WASHINGTON, D.C. ACCOMPANYING HIM WAS PRESIDENT GEORGE WASHINGTON.

L'ENFANT POINTED TO THE HILL AND EXCLAIMED,

I COULD DISCOVER NO ONE (LOCATION)... TO GREET THE CONGRESSIONAL BUILDING AS THAT ON THE WEST END OF JENKINS HEIGHTS. IT STANDS AS A PEDESTAL WAITING FOR A MONUMENT!

THAT IS HOW THE SITE WAS SELECTED FOR THE UNITED STATES **CAPITOL.**

Capitol Hill is one of the most famous neighborhoods in the world. It is bounded on the north by F Street NE, on the south by the Southwest Freeway, and on the east by 14th Street SE and NE. Of course, being the land of politicians, nobody can agree on its western boundary, which is vaguely described as somewhere down the Mall from the Capitol.

THE SELF-PROCLAIMED ARCHITECT

WILLIAM THORNTON WAS BORN ON THE ISLAND OF JOST VAN DYKE IN THE VIRGIN ISLANDS IN 1759.

HIS PARENTS WERE WEALTHY QUAKERS WHO COULD AFFORD TO SEND HIM TO MEDICAL SCHOOL IN SCOTLAND.

AFTER GRADUATING, HE USED MORE OF HIS DADDY'S MONEY TO GO ON A GRAND TOUR.

IN PARIS DR. THORNTON DABBLED IN ART AND TRIED HIS HAND AT INVENTING.

HE SETTLED IN PHILA-DELPHIA, PA. AROUND 1787 AND MARRIED A 15 YEAR-OLD GIRL.

A SHORT TIME LATER THORNTON ENTERED A CONTEST TO DESIGN A LIBRARY AND WON. NOW HE FANCIED HIMSELF AN ARCHITECT.

ONE DAY IN THE AUTUMN OF 1792 DOCTOR THORNTON SAW AN ADVERTISE-MENT IN AN OLD NEWS-PAPER...

THERE'S A **CONTEST** TO DESIGN THE **CAPITOL** BUILDING FOR THE NEW FEDERAL CITY.

Publick Ledger

BUT, THE DEADLINE WAS **THREE MONTHS AGO.**

SO WHAT! I'LL ENTER IT ANYWAY!

WHAT FOLLOWS IS THE STORY OF HOW A RANK AMATEUR DESIGNED THE CAPITOL OF THE UNITED STATES.

Although he was a licensed physician, medicine was just a sideline for Dr. William Thornton. For example, he had experimented with steam-driven paddle boats long before Robert Fulton.

He also had a knack for picking winning race horses and used his winnings to buy a stable of some of the fastest thoroughbreds in the United States.

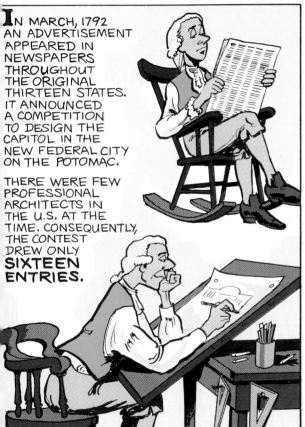

IN MARCH, 1792 AN ADVERTISEMENT APPEARED IN NEWSPAPERS THROUGHOUT THE ORIGINAL THIRTEEN STATES. IT ANNOUNCED A COMPETITION TO DESIGN THE CAPITOL IN THE NEW FEDERAL CITY ON THE POTOMAC.

THERE WERE FEW PROFESSIONAL ARCHITECTS IN THE U.S. AT THE TIME. CONSEQUENTLY, THE CONTEST DREW ONLY **SIXTEEN ENTRIES.**

BACK IN THE NATION'S CAPITAL, PHILADELPHIA, PA., THE THREE COMMISSIONERS FOR THE NEW CENTER OF GOVERNMENT WENT OVER THE ENTRIES.

PRESIDENT WASHINGTON AND HIS SECRETARY OF STATE, THOMAS JEFFERSON, SERVED AS CONSULTANTS. JEFFERSON WAS A RESPECTED AMATEUR ARCHITECT.

THEY'RE ALL TERRIBLE!

THIS DESIGN BY STEPHEN HALLET LOOKS PROMISING.

LET'S HAVE HIM SUBMIT ANOTHER.

HERE'S A REQUEST BY A DOCTOR THORNTON TO SUBMIT A DESIGN **BUT,** THE DEADLINE WAS THREE MONTHS AGO!

SO LET HIM ENTER. WHAT HAVE WE GOT TO LOSE?

61

Some guidelines for this competition were as follows: the Capitol was to contain a Representatives Hall and a conference room, each with a capacity for 300, a Senate room of 1,200 square feet and twelve additional rooms of 6,000 square feet each.

The President's Choice

STEPHEN HALLET WAS A 37 YEAR-OLD PROFESSIONAL ARCHITECT FROM FRANCE WHO ENTERED THE COMPETITION TO DESIGN THE U.S. CAPITOL. THE CAPITAL COMMISSIONERS WANTED SOME CHANGES, SO HALLET DELIVERED A SECOND SET OF PLANS IN DECEMBER, 1792.

LOOKS GREAT!

VERY NI-I-CE!

THE PRIZE IS VIRTUALLY YOURS, MR. HALLET.

MEANWHILE, **DR. WILLIAM THORNTON** HAD PRESENTED A LATE ENTRY AND WAS ASKED TO SUBMIT ANOTHER...

WHICH HE DID IN JANUARY, 1792.

HALLET'S DESIGN IS MUCH BETTER.

I DON-N'T KNO-O-W...

HM-M-M...

I LIKE IT!

THE DOCTOR'S DESIGN HAS GRANDEUR, SIMPLICITY, AND BEAUTY.

PRESIDENT WASHINGTON'S OPINION CLINCHED IT FOR DOCTOR THORNTON.

REALIZING THEY HAD *MISLED* HALLET, THOMAS JEFFERSON PROCEEDED TO MAKE AMENDS.

WE'LL **PAY** YOU FOR YOUR DESIGNS AND...

WE'LL PUT YOU IN CHARGE OF CONSTRUCTING THE CAPITOL!

Dr. Thornton went on to design other buildings in Washington including St. John's Church at 3240 O Street NW in Georgetown, the Octagon House at 1799 New York Avenue NW, and Tudor Place at 1644 31st NW.

For a while, Dr. Thornton lived at 1321 F Street NW. The site is now occupied by an office building. His permanent residence was at 3219 M Street NW.

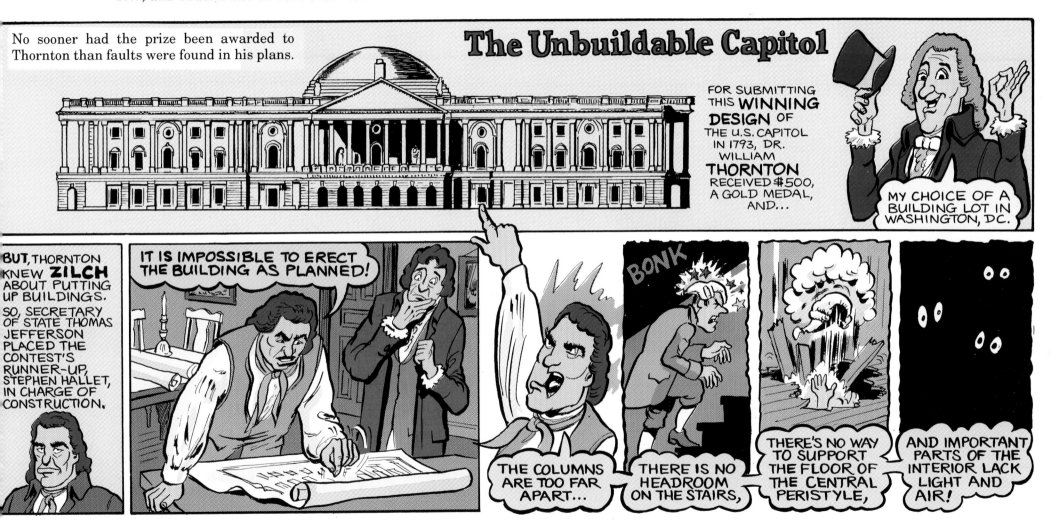

No sooner had the prize been awarded to Thornton than faults were found in his plans.

The Unbuildable Capitol

FOR SUBMITTING THIS **WINNING DESIGN** OF THE U.S. CAPITOL IN 1793, DR. WILLIAM **THORNTON** RECEIVED $500, A GOLD MEDAL, AND...

MY CHOICE OF A BUILDING LOT IN WASHINGTON, D.C.

BUT, THORNTON KNEW **ZILCH** ABOUT PUTTING UP BUILDINGS. SO, SECRETARY OF STATE THOMAS JEFFERSON PLACED THE CONTEST'S RUNNER-UP, STEPHEN HALLET, IN CHARGE OF CONSTRUCTION.

IT IS IMPOSSIBLE TO ERECT THE BUILDING AS PLANNED!

THE COLUMNS ARE TOO FAR APART...

BONK

THERE IS NO HEADROOM ON THE STAIRS,

THERE'S NO WAY TO SUPPORT THE FLOOR OF THE CENTRAL PERISTYLE,

AND IMPORTANT PARTS OF THE INTERIOR LACK LIGHT AND AIR!

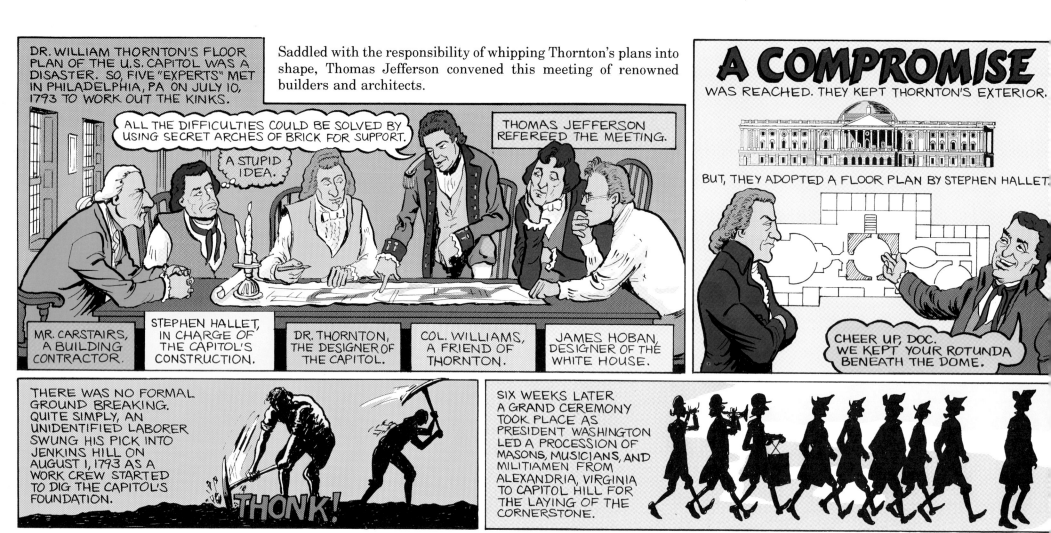

DR. WILLIAM THORNTON'S FLOOR PLAN OF THE U.S. CAPITOL WAS A DISASTER. SO, FIVE "EXPERTS" MET IN PHILADELPHIA, PA ON JULY 10, 1793 TO WORK OUT THE KINKS.

Saddled with the responsibility of whipping Thornton's plans into shape, Thomas Jefferson convened this meeting of renowned builders and architects.

ALL THE DIFFICULTIES COULD BE SOLVED BY USING SECRET ARCHES OF BRICK FOR SUPPORT.

A STUPID IDEA.

THOMAS JEFFERSON REFEREED THE MEETING.

MR. CARSTAIRS, A BUILDING CONTRACTOR.

STEPHEN HALLET, IN CHARGE OF THE CAPITOL'S CONSTRUCTION.

DR. THORNTON, THE DESIGNER OF THE CAPITOL.

COL. WILLIAMS, A FRIEND OF THORNTON.

JAMES HOBAN, DESIGNER OF THE WHITE HOUSE.

A COMPROMISE

WAS REACHED. THEY KEPT THORNTON'S EXTERIOR.

BUT, THEY ADOPTED A FLOOR PLAN BY STEPHEN HALLET.

CHEER UP, DOC. WE KEPT YOUR ROTUNDA BENEATH THE DOME.

THERE WAS NO FORMAL GROUND BREAKING. QUITE SIMPLY, AN UNIDENTIFIED LABORER SWUNG HIS PICK INTO JENKINS HILL ON AUGUST 1, 1793 AS A WORK CREW STARTED TO DIG THE CAPITOL'S FOUNDATION.

THONK!

SIX WEEKS LATER A GRAND CEREMONY TOOK PLACE AS PRESIDENT WASHINGTON LED A PROCESSION OF MASONS, MUSICIANS, AND MILITIAMEN FROM ALEXANDRIA, VIRGINIA TO CAPITOL HILL FOR THE LAYING OF THE CORNERSTONE.

Stephen Hallet was the first professional architect to work on the Capitol. In 1786 he was one of three architects listed in the *Almanack Royale of Paris*.

THE CORNERSTONE

OF THE U.S. CAPITOL WAS CEMENTED INTO PLACE BY PRESIDENT GEORGE WASHINGTON ON SEPTEMBER 18, 1793. AS ACTING GRAND MASTER OF MARYLAND'S LODGE OF ANCIENT FREE AND ACCEPTED MASONS, WASHINGTON WORE THE SASH, COLLAR, AND APRON OF THE MASONS.

WASHINGTON PLACED A SILVER PLATE WITH THE DATE ON THE STONE. TODAY, NOBODY CAN FIND THE EXACT LOCATION OF THIS CORNERSTONE IN THE CAPITOL.

IT WAS A SOLEMN MASONIC CEREMONY. THESE MEN HELD ITEMS THAT THE PRESIDENT SPRINKLED ON THE CORNERSTONE: CORN, THE SYMBOL OF *PLENTY*; WINE FOR THE *HEALTH* OF THE WORKERS; AND OIL FOR *EVERLASTING PEACE*.

65

Hallet's main problem was that he refused to show his revisions of Thornton's plans to anyone, not even the commissioners. He would tell the stonemasons what to do but never show them the plans. Moreover, he insisted on being credited as the *original inventor* of the Capitol.

CONSTRUCTION

OF THE U.S. CAPITOL BEGAN IN SEPTEMBER, 1793.

THE ARCHITECT, DR. WILLIAM THORNTON, HAD OVERALL SUPERVISION.

STEPHEN HALLET WAS IN CHARGE OF THE ACTUAL CONSTRUCTION.

STILL BITTER BECAUSE HIS DESIGN FOR THE CAPITOL WAS NOT ACCEPTED, MR. HALLET PROMPTLY MADE HIS OWN CHANGES.

HE REPLACED THORNTON'S ROTUNDA WITH A SQUARE COURTYARD.

WHEN PRESIDENT WASHINGTON SAW IT, HE "EXPRESSED HIS DISAPPROVAL WITH WARMTH..."

MISTAH HALLET, THAT'S NOT WHAT WE ALL HAD IN MI-I-IND.

ON THE OTHER HAND, THE DISTRICT OF COLUMBIA COMMISSIONERS GAVE HIM A STRONG REPRIMAND.

IF THAT'S HOW YOU FEEL, I QUIT!

YOUR RESIGNATION IS REFUSED... YOU'RE FIRED!

HALLET LEFT, BUT TOOK THE PLANS WITH HIM.

THE DISTRICT HAD TO SUE HIM TO GET THEM BACK.

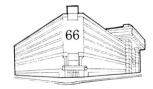

66

By late summer, 1793, a yellow fever epidemic hit Philadelphia, then the U. S. capital. It would kill ten percent of the city's population. Coincidently, to "escape the heat," President Washington left the City of Brotherly Love for Mount Vernon. His cabinet officers moved to the outskirts of Philly and continued to conduct the nation's business. Only Alexander Hamilton came down with the disease.

After his dismissal on November 15, 1794, Stephen Hallet was replaced by **James Hoban** as Superintendent of Construction of the U. S. Capitol.

HOBAN, THE ARCHITECT OF THE WHITE HOUSE, NOW HAD THE RESPONSIBILITY FOR ERECTING BOTH BUILDINGS.

PART OF HOBAN'S CREW CONTINUED TO WORK ON THE WHITE HOUSE WHILE THE OTHERS RIPPED OUT THE CAPITOL'S FOUNDATION AND PREPARED TO START OVER.

LABOR SHORTAGE

FROM THE OUTSET, HOBAN'S BIGGEST HEADACHE WAS THE SHORTAGE OF SKILLED CRAFTSMEN. THE MASTER STONEMASON WAS A 65 YEAR-OLD SCOTSMAN NAMED COLLEN WILLIAMSON. HE TRAINED 25 HIRED SLAVES TO CUT THE ROUGH FOUNDATION STONES.

AT THE TIME THE YOUNG UNITED STATES WAS ENJOYING AN ERA OF PROSPERITY, AND SPECIALISTS IN THE BUILDING TRADES WERE IN GREAT DEMAND IN THE BIG CITIES.

LEAVE A HIGH-PAYIN' JOB TA WORK FER PITTANCE? YE GA-A-T T' BE **DAFT!**

YE'D NOT GET ME T' WORK IN THAT BUG INFESTED SWAMP ON THE POTOMAC!

Collen Williamson was a poor manager, unable to keep his men working to the maximum. He hated almost everybody, particularly the Irish, Catholics, and Blacks. Superintendent Hoban, an Irishman, was a frequent target of Collen's prejudice. Williamson called Hoban an amateur to his face, among other insults.

The Commissioners and Hoban finally had enough of Williamson's constant griping and inefficiency. They fired him in the spring of 1795.

The first *Goodwill Ambassador and Promoter of Washington, DC* was **George Walker**, self-styled "Citizen of the World." Born in Scotland, he moved to Philadelphia and became a successful merchant before moving to Georgetown, MD.

Believing the new capital would "rise to commercial importance," he paid 10,140 American pounds (about $27,000) for 358 acres in 1789.

Mr. Walker's property in Washington was a five-block wide swath that extended from the Eastern Branch all the way up to 5th and G Streets Northeast.

THE SCOTTISH STONEMASONS

AROUND 1792 MR. WALKER PRODUCED A BROCHURE THAT TOUTED THE BENEFITS OF INVESTING IN THE NEW CAPITAL CITY. HE PLANNED TO VISIT ENGLAND AND DISTRIBUTE IT IN LONDON TO ATTRACT BRITISH SPECULATORS.

SIR, TWO GENTLEMEN TO SEE YOU.

EARLY IN 1793 THE DISTRICT COMMISSIONERS LEARNED THAT WALKER WAS PLANNING A TRIP TO HIS OLD HOMELAND. STYMIED BY A LABOR SHORTAGE, THEY DECIDED TO SOLICIT HIS HELP.

WE'D LIKE YOU TO RECRUIT 50 TO 100 STONEMASONS FROM GREAT BRITAIN.

WALKER STRUCK OUT IN LONDON BUT HIS LUCK CHANGED IN SCOTLAND.

EDINBURGH'S BUILDING BOOM HAD GONE BUST AND MEN WERE LOOKING FOR WORK. THEY WERE EVEN WILLING TO RELOCATE IN AMERICA.

WALKER'S RECRUITS STARTED TO ARRIVE IN WASHINGTON IN THE SPRING OF 1794. THE FIRST WERE GEORGE THOMSON, JAMES WHITE, ALEXANDER WILSON, ALEXANDER SCOTT, JAMES McINTOSH, AND ROBERT BROWN.

These stonemasons founded St. Andrew's Presbyterian Church which existed for about ten years. It was one of the first congregations founded in D.C.

In London, John Trumbull, the famous artist, working as secretary to Special Ambassador John Jay, heard that the U.S. capital city needed an architect-builder. Trumbull told his friend, George Hadfield, to apply for the job. Trumbull then wrote a letter of recommendation on Hadfield's behalf to Tobias Lear, President Washington's secretary. Washington and Lear forwarded the letter to the Commissioners.

THE U.S. CAPITOL WAS SLOWLY TAKING SHAPE IN 1795.

ON OCTOBER 15 **GEORGE HADFIELD,** AN ENGLISH ARCHITECT, BECAME THE BUILDING'S **THIRD** SUPERVISOR OF CONSTRUCTION.

FROM THE OUTSET, HADFIELD LOCKED HORNS WITH THE ARCHITECT OF THE CAPITOL, DR. WILLIAM **THORNTON.**

IT NEEDS AN **ATTIC!**

YER HEAD NEEDS AN **ATTIC!**

I AM WRITING MY OBJECTIONS TO THE **PRESIDENT!**

IDIOT...

TELL MR. HADFIELD TO KEEP HIS OPINIONS TO HIMSELF.

HADFIELD'S REACTION...

I QUIT!

A FEW DAYS LATER, HE RECONSIDERED.

I WITHDRAW MY RESIGNATION.

HADFIELD STAYED ON THE JOB FOR THREE YEARS. THEN, HE REFUSED TO TURN OVER THE PLANS FOR THE EXECUTIVE OFFICES. SO...

THE COMMISSIONERS FIRED HIM IN 1798 AND GAVE HIM SHIP FARE TO ENGLAND.

Had anyone ever checked Hadfield's background, they would have found out that he had never supervised the construction of any large building.

69

AFTER GEORGE HADFIELD WAS FIRED IN 1798, JAMES **HOBAN** TOOK OVER AS THE CONSTRUCTION BOSS NOT ONLY OF THE U.S. CAPITOL, BUT THE WHITE HOUSE AS WELL.

Instead of buying specific quantities of stone for each building in the capital, the commissioners purchased the entire Aquia Creek quarry in Stafford County, Virginia from George Brent. Brent's brother, Daniel, was married to Commissioner Carroll's sister.

THE COMMISSIONERS EMPLOYED 25 SLAVES IN THE QUARRY.

THE GREATEST SOURCE OF TIMBER WAS THE WHITE OAK SWAMP NEAR MOUNT VERNON AND THE LEE PLANTATION IN WESTMORELAND COUNTY, VIRGINIA.

WHERE THE MATERIAL CAME FROM
TO BUILD THE U.S. CAPITOL AND THE WHITE HOUSE

THIS ARKOSE SANDSTONE WAS FLOATED 40 MILES UP THE POTOMAC TO WASHINGTON.

JEREMIAH KALE, THE MASTER BRICKMAKER, FOUND THE SOIL IN THE CITY TO BE IDEAL FOR MAKING **BRICKS.** THREE KILNS WERE SET UP TO MAKE THE ENORMOUS QUANTITY THAT WOULD BE REQUIRED FOR THE INNER WALLS OF THE FEDERAL BUILDINGS.

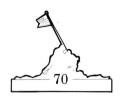

The heavy carpentry was in the hands of Peter Lennox while Joseph Middleton did the finish work. Middleton also built the window and doors including those in the great state rooms.

BY THE SPRING OF 1799 CONSTRUCTION OF WASHINGTON, D.C. WAS HOPELESSLY BEHIND SCHEDULE. ON CAPITOL HILL, ONLY THE SENATE WING WAS STANDING.

JAMES HOBAN WAS STILL THE SUPERINTENDENT OF CONSTRUCTION.

GEORGE BLAGDEN HAD BEEN GIVEN THE CONTRACT TO OVERSEE THE FINISHING OF THE STONE WORK.

JOHN KEARNEY HAD THE PLASTERING CONTRACT FOR THE CAPITOL.

WILSON BRYAN WAS APPOINTED SUPERINTENDENT OF CARPENTERS.

THE YEAR 1800 WAS SET BY LAW FOR THE GOVERNMENT TO TAKE ITS SEAT IN WASHINGTON, BUT...

THERE WERE PROBLEMS IN THE SENATE CHAMBER.

THE ROOF LEAKS!

THE PAINTING CONTRACTOR, LEWIS CLEPHANE, WAS ORDERED TO PUT ANOTHER COAT OF SAND PAINT ON THE SHINGLED ROOF.

READY OR NOT, IN THE AUTUMN OF 1800, THE GOVERNMENT MOVED BAG AND BAGGAGE FROM ITS TEMPORARY SEAT IN PHILADELPHIA TO WASHINGTON.

Orlando Cooke, a slater, and John Emory, a plumber, both from Philadelphia, were contracted in 1797 to complete the roof. Although they were paid, their workmanship was so bad that they were called back again and again to patch the leaks and fix the lead work in the gutters.

71

President John Adams came to the Senate Chamber on November 22, 1800 to address the first joint session in the Capitol. Not until Woodrow Wilson in 1913 would another President address Congress in person.

The federal government opened for business in Washington on November 17, 1800.

ONLY THE SENATE WING OF THE U.S. CAPITOL WAS READY.

THE OVEN

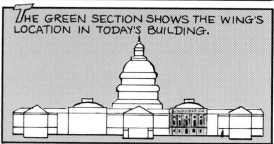
THE GREEN SECTION SHOWS THE WING'S LOCATION IN TODAY'S BUILDING.

THE STRUCTURE WAS CROWDED WITH 32 SENATORS, 106 REPRESENTATIVES, THE SUPREME COURT, THE CIRCUIT COURT, AND THE LIBRARY OF CONGRESS.

GET OUTA MY SEAT!

THIS IS THE SENATE AN' IT'S MAH SEAT!

COME TO ORDER!

WHERE'S THE LIBRARY?

SUPREME COURT? TRY THE CELLAR.

I MOVE FOR A VOTE.

2-I-2

LET'S GO TO LUNCH.

TO RELIEVE CONGESTION, A BRICK, OVAL-SHAPED BUILDING WAS PUT UP FOR THE HOUSE OF REPRESENTATIVES IN THE WINTER OF 1801.

A COVERED WALKWAY CONNECTED IT TO THE SENATE.

THE TEMPORARY BUILDING GOT SO HOT IN THE SUMMER THAT THE CONGRESSMEN CALLED IT *THE OVEN.*

BENJAMIN HENRY LATROBE

WAS A LONDON-TRAINED ARCHITECT WORKING IN PHILADELPHIA. HE HAD DESIGNED BUILDINGS ALL OVER THE EAST COAST OF EARLY AMERICA.

PRESIDENT THOMAS JEFFERSON SUMMONED HIM TO WASHINGTON IN 1802 TO DESIGN A DRY DOCK FOR THE NAVY YARD.

Latrobe designed a huge covered drydock where ships of the United States Navy would be mothballed. It was never built but Jefferson was very impressed with Latrobe's work.

EARLY IN 1803 JAMES HOBAN CALLED ON MR. JEFFERSON.

I'M OVERWORKED AND UNDERPAID AS ARCHITECT OF BOTH THE CAPITOL AND THE PRESIDENT'S HOUSE.

FINE! YOU'RE RELIEVED OF THE CAPITOL JOB.

ONE OF LATROBE'S FIRST ACTIONS WAS TO HIRE ANOTHER ARCHITECT, **JOHN LENTHALL**, TO MANAGE THE DAY-TO-DAY CONSTRUCTION.

TEAR THE OVEN DOWN AND START BUILDING THE SOUTH WING.

✺ THE TEMPORARY CONGRESSIONAL CHAMBERS.

ON MARCH 6, 1803 JEFFERSON APPOINTED LATROBE "SURVEYOR OF PUBLIC BUILDINGS," MEANING HE WAS IN CHARGE OF CONSTRUCTING THE U.S. CAPITOL.

THORNTON'S ✺ PLANS ARE AWFUL

✺ THE DESIGNER OF THE CAPITOL.

LATROBE IMMEDIATELY LEFT TOWN TO WORK ON ONE OF HIS MANY ON-GOING COMMISSIONS THAT HE CONSIDERED JUST AS IMPORTANT AS THE CAPITOL—THE CHESAPEAKE AND DELAWARE CANAL.

Benjamin Latrobe was one of America's foremost architects of his time. His masterpieces include the Roman Catholic Cathedral in Baltimore, the Bank of Pennsylvania in Philadelphia and the Philadelphia Waterworks, the nation's first steam-powered waterworks.

LATROBE'S CHANGES

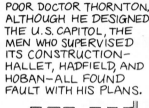

POOR DOCTOR THORNTON, ALTHOUGH HE DESIGNED THE U.S. CAPITOL, THE MEN WHO SUPERVISED ITS CONSTRUCTION—HALLET, HADFIELD, AND HOBAN—ALL FOUND FAULT WITH HIS PLANS.

NOW, BENJAMIN LATROBE WANTS TO CHANGE MY ELLIPTICAL-SHAPED HOUSE OF REPRESENTATIVES CHAMBER.

IN 1804 LATROBE SHOWED HIS VERSION OF THE CAPITOL TO PRESIDENT THOMAS JEFFERSON.

THE CONGRESSIONAL CHAMBER WILL BE TWO SEMI-CIRCLES ABUTTING A PARALLELOGRAM, AND IT WILL BE ON THE SECOND FLOOR INSTEAD OF THE GROUND FLOOR!

THORNTON'S SOUTH WING HAD JUST ONE BIG ROOM. WE'LL GO WITH YOUR PLANS.

BY SUMMER, 1804 THE HOUSE, OR SOUTH, WING REACHED TO THE HEIGHT OF THE SECOND FLOOR. LATROBE PLANNED FOR COMMITTEE ROOMS, OFFICES, AND STORAGE SPACES ON THE GROUND FLOOR.

DOCTOR THORNTON, I REVISED THE FRONT ENTRANCE. IT'LL BE ON THE **EAST SIDE**.

WHAT?!?

I DESIGNED THE CAPITOL TO FACE THE PRESIDENT'S HOUSE **TO THE WEST!**

LET'S LET THE PRESIDENT DECIDE.

IT'LL FACE **EAST!**

I'M GETTING AN ULCER.

THERE IS **NO** EXPLANATION OF **WHY** THE U.S. CAPITOL FACES EAST.

The south wing of the U. S. Capitol was completed in 1807. It was connected to the Senate, or north wing, by a corridor made of rough boards.

THE ECHO CHAMBER

THE HOUSE OF REPRESENTATIVES MET HERE FOR THE FIRST TIME ON OCTOBER 26, 1807. BUT, AS SOON AS SPEAKER JOSEPH VARNUM OF MASSACHUSETTS OPENED THE SESSION, THE MEMBERS REALIZED THEY WERE IN AN **ACCOUSTICAL FIASCO.**

THE TE-E-NTH CONGRESS OF THE U-NAH-TED STA-A-TES WILL COME TO **OR-DAH!**

THEY HUNG CURTAINS AND RAISED THE FLOOR. NOTHING WORKED. FINALLY, IN 1850...

THE BILL TO APPROPRIATE $100,000 TO EXTEND THE CAPITOL AND BUILD A **NEW** HOUSE CHAMBER PASSES!

AFTER A NOISY HALF-CENTURY, CONGRESS RECONVENED IN THEIR NEW, *ECHOLESS* CHAMBER IN DECEMBER, 1857.

Among Latrobe's innovations were the "capitals," or tops, of the columns in the stairs of the Senate vestibule. Latrobe had native corn carved on these capitals by two young sculptors from Italy, Guiseppe Frangoni and Giavanni Andrei.

John Lenthall constantly urged Latrobe to move permanently to Washington, DC, but the architect kept refusing. Considering his work on the Chesapeake and Delaware Canal more important, Latrobe lived in Philadelphia, then in Delaware at New Castle and Wilmington.

The Absentee Architect

AFTER TAKING OVER AS ARCHITECT OF THE U.S. CAPITOL, BENJAMIN LATROBE COMPLETED THE SOUTH, OR CONGRESSIONAL, WING IN 1806. MEANWHILE, THE SENATE WING NEEDED REPAIRS.

THE ROOF LEAKS AND THE PLASTER'S FALLING.

I'VE GOT AN IDEA. LET'S GUT IT AND START OVER!

LATROBE ORDERED HIS CONSTRUCTION FOREMAN, JOHN LENTHALL, TO RIP OUT THE INTERIOR OF THE SENATE WING. THEN THEY RAISED THE MAIN FLOOR AND BUILT THE SUPREME COURT CHAMBERS UNDERNEATH.

THOSE ARCHES LOOK WEAK. I BETTER TELL MR. LATROBE.

LATROBE WAS SELDOM IN WASHINGTON BECAUSE HE WAS BUSY WITH OTHER JOBS SUCH AS ERECTING THE ROMAN CATHOLIC CATHEDRAL IN BALTIMORE.

HIS SUPERVISION OF THE CAPITOL WAS DONE BY WRITING TO LENTHALL.

AROUND 1808 CONGRESS COMPLAINED ABOUT LATROBE'S LONG ABSENCES.

THE WORK ON THE CAPITOL IS GOING TOO SLOW.

THAT'S BECAUSE LATROBE IS NEVER HERE TO SUPERVISE!

LATROBE RETORTED,

CONGRESS SLOWS THE PACE BY THEIR CONSTANT NIT-PICKING EVERY CONSTRUCTION DETAIL.

The Capitol was designed to house two branches of government, the Legislative and the Judicial. It was Latrobe's job to make a home for the Supreme Court in the Capitol.

The Judiciary Act of 1789 required the U. S. Supreme Court Justices to travel twice a year to remote areas of the country and preside over Circuit Courts.

A Most Miserable Job

THE PURPOSE WAS TO ACQUAINT AMERICANS WITH THEIR NEW **SUPREME COURT.**

THE JUSTICES ALSO BECAME AWARE OF LOCAL OPINION AND STATE LAWS.

C'MON, JUDGE, PUSH!

AT TIMES THE JUSTICES SPENT UP TO 19 HOURS A DAY ON LOUSY ROADS OF ROCKS, RUTS, AND MUD.

BRUISED AND EXHAUSTED AFTER BOUNCING INSIDE A STAGECOACH, JUDGES OFTEN ARRIVED AT THE CIRCUIT COURT TOO SICK TO CONDUCT ANY BUSINESS.

THEIR NIGHTS WERE SPENT IN WHAT WE NOW CONSIDER AS QUAINT OLD INNS, WHICH WERE REALLY SMELLY, OVERCROWDED FLOPHOUSES. JUSTICE IREDELL SUMMED UP HIS LIFE...

I FEEL LIKE A TRAVELING POSTBOY.

THE JUDGES COMPLAINED TO PRESIDENT WASHINGTON IN 1792.

TELL HIM WE'RE GOING TO QUIT!

WASHINGTON SENT THE LETTER TO CONGRESS, WHO RELENTED IN 1793: ONE CIRCUIT TRIP A YEAR WOULD BE ENOUGH.

When the Constitution of the United States went into effect in 1789, New York was the nation's capital.

THE SUPREME COURT OF THE U.S. MET FOR THE FIRST TIME IN THE ROYAL EXCHANGE BUILDING ON BROAD STREET IN NEW YORK CITY ON FEBRUARY 1, 1790.

PRESIDENT WASHINGTON HAD APPOINTED SIX JUSTICES, BUT ONLY THREE SHOWED UP FOR THE OPENING SESSION: WILLIAM CUSHING OF MASSACHUSETTS, CHIEF JUSTICE JOHN JAY OF NEW YORK, AND JAMES WILSON OF PENNSYLVANIA. THIS POOR ATTENDANCE DID NOT MATTER BECAUSE THE COURT HAD PRACTICALLY NO BUSINESS DURING ITS FIRST THREE YEARS.

PHILADELPHIA BECAME THE CAPITAL THE FOLLOWING YEAR AND THE COURT HELD ITS FEBRUARY SESSION IN AN UNHEATED ROOM AT INDEPENDENCE HALL.

NEW SPACE WAS FOUND IN CITY HALL, BUT THE JUSTICES HAD TO SHARE IT WITH THE MAYOR'S COURT FOR THE NEXT TEN YEARS.

WHEN THE JUSTICES ARRIVED AT THE NEWLY CONSTRUCTED CAPITAL, WASHINGTON, D.C., THEY RECEIVED SOME UNSETTLING NEWS.

ER... AH-H...NOBODY THOUGHT TO GIVE YOU A BUILDING.

IT'S ALL CONGRESS' FAULT.

ALREADY THEY'RE FOULING THINGS UP

DRAT!

IT WOULD BE ANOTHER 135 YEARS BEFORE THE SUPREME COURT GOT ITS OWN BUILDING.

Meanwhile, the Justices would hold court in the Capitol's basement.

Latrobe continued to revise Thornton's plans.
Thornton reacted by smearing Latrobe in the newspapers.

Meanwhile, Congress was anxious to have a home, so they appropriated another $50,000 for the Capitol, then $110,000 more.

Death in the Supreme Court

CONGRESS WAS COMPLAINING THAT THE CONSTRUCTION OF THE U.S. CAPITOL WAS GOING TOO SLOW IN 1806.

RUMBLE RUMBLE CRUMPF!

WHA' WAZZAT?

TO SPEED THINGS UP, BEN LATROBE THE ARCHITECT, ALLOWED HIS FOREMAN, JOHN LENTHALL, TO REMOVE THE SUPPORTS OF THE ARCHED CEILINGS SOONER THAN NORMAL... BUT THE CEMENT HAD NOT COMPLETELY HARDENED.

CR-REAK-SCRAPE

LOOK OUT!

RUMBLE-CRASH

WHUMP

LENTHALL WROTE TO HIS BOSS ABOUT THE PROBLEM. LATROBE RESPONDED,

...SORRY THE ARCHES HAVE FALLEN, BUT I HAVE HAD THESE ACCIDENTS BEFORE ON A LARGER SCALE.

(WE) MUST THEREFORE GRIN AND BEAR IT!

ON SEPT. 21, 1808 LENTHALL WAS REMOVING THE BRACES FROM AN ARCH IN THE LOWER LEVEL OF THE SENATE BUILDING WHERE THE SUPREME COURT WOULD HOLD THEIR MEETINGS.

AGAIN, THE CEMENT HAD NOT COMPLETELY HARDENED. THE ARCH COLLAPSED, KILLING LENTHALL.

LATROBE DETERMINED THAT HASTE AND CHEAP MATERIAL CAUSED THE ACCIDENT.

FROM NOW ON I WILL BUILD THE CAPITOL AT MY OWN PACE WITH THE BEST MATERIAL.

Another problem at the Capitol was leaky skylights in the dome. Jefferson wanted fancy glass. Latrobe objected, saying they would leak and blind people on sunny days.

President Jefferson pulled rank and overruled Latrobe. The fancy glass was installed and, sure enough, the dome leaked.

By 1807 there was a public outcry over cost overruns, but the money kept flowing and the work continued.

A MATTER OF PRIORITIES

BEN LATROBE MOVED HIS FAMILY FROM PHILADELPHIA, PA TO WASHINGTON, DC IN 1808.

MEANWHILE LATROBE LOST SEVERAL ARCHITECTURAL JOBS INCLUDING THE CHESAPEAKE AND DELAWARE CANAL. HE WAS FORCED TO DECLARE BANKRUPTCY.

THEN HIS FOREMAN, J. LENTHALL, WAS KILLED WHEN AN ARCH COLLAPSED IN THE CAPITOL.

THESE FACTORS CONVINCED HIM TO SPEND ALL HIS TIME AND ENERGY ON THE CAPITOL. SOON BOTH WINGS WERE COMPLETED.

HE WAS ABOUT TO START ON THE CENTRAL SECTION IN 1811, BUT...

ANOTHER WAR WITH GREAT BRITAIN SEEMED IMMINENT, SO CONGRESS DECIDED TO RESHUFFLE ITS SPENDING.

CONGRESS REGRETS TO INFORM YOU, MR. LATROBE, THAT FUNDING FOR THE CAPITOL HAS CEASED. YOUR SERVICES WILL NO LONGER BE NEEDED UNTIL FURTHER NOTICE.

THE GOVERNMENT PUT ITS MONEY INTO DEFENSE. ON JUNE 18, 1812 CONGRESS DECLARED WAR AGAINST GREAT BRITAIN, KICKING OFF **THE WAR OF 1812.**

For two years the fighting took place far from Washington. Then, in the summer of 1814, a British squadron under Rear Admiral Sir George Cockburn landed soldiers and marines near Benedict on Maryland's Western Shore.

Section Four

Destruction and Rebuilding

The ongoing battles among the politicians of Washington were rudely interrupted when the British burned the place down during the War of 1812. Out of the ashes came a new capital city crowned by the *Statue of Freedom* on top of the U. S. Capitol.

An American force of Regular Army, Marines, Pennsylvania Dragoons, and Maryland Militia set up a blocking position at Bladensburg, Maryland on August 14, 1814.

The Americans put up a fierce fight, but the better trained and disciplined British managed to outflank them. The Yanks fell back leaving the British with a clear lane to the capital.

By late afternoon, most people--residents and politicians alike, had left town.

THE 3rd BRIGADE,

CONSISTING OF BRITISH SEAMEN, MARINES, AND MOST OF THE 21st REGIMENT OF FOOT (INFANTRY)— SOME 1,460 MEN, MARCHED INTO WASHINGTON AT 8 PM ON AUGUST 24, 1814.

THEY STOPPED AT THE CAPITOL AND FIRED INTO THE WINDOWS TO DISCOURAGE SNIPERS. LT. DE LACY EVANS LED A GROUP THAT BROKE DOWN THE DOORS.

INSIDE THEY ROAMED AROUND LIKE TOURISTS. A FEW SOLDIERS STOLE PAINTINGS AND OTHER SOUVENIRS.

MEANWHILE...

ADMIRAL COCKBURN, WHAT ARE YOUR ORDERS?

SET CHARGES, GENERAL ROSS, AND **BLOW IT UP!**

WHAT?!

THE EXPLOSION WILL DAMAGE OUR HOMES!

CONVINCED THAT HE HAD NO QUARREL WITH THE CIVILIANS, COCKBURN TOOK A DIFFERENT TACK.

LIEUTENANT PRATT, YOU'RE AN EXPERT IN THIS BUSINESS. **BURN IT DOWN!**

PRATT'S MEN TRIED TO START A FIRE BY SHOOTING ROCKETS INTO THE CEILING. NOTHING HAPPENED BECAUSE IT WAS COVERED WITH SHEET IRON. CONT'D.

BAM! BAM!

WHOOSH! WHOOSHSHSH!

Before they torched the Capitol, some of the British soldiers did some looting. Admiral Cockburn took a small bound copy of a Treasury report as a souvenir. Others swiped the paintings of Louis XVI and Marie Antoinette that hung in the room next to the Senate Chamber.

AUGUST 24, 1814 – THE BRITISH COULD NOT SET THE U.S. CAPITOL ON FIRE BY SHOOTING ROCKETS INTO THE CEILING.

Lieutenant Pratt's men started to pile furniture in the middle chambers of the House and Senate.

THE BURNING

THEY ADDED GUNPOWDER...

THEN FIRED ROCKETS INTO THE PILE.

SOON BOTH WINGS WERE ABLAZE.
INSIDE THERE WAS PLENTY TO BURN:

740 BOOKS PURCHASED IN EUROPE IN 1802 AS THE NUCLEUS FOR THE LIBRARY OF CONGRESS,

THE SECRET JOURNAL OF CONGRESS, CAREFULLY LOCKED IN A SPECIAL DRAWER,

AND THE CLOCK OVER THE SPEAKER'S CHAIR. WHEN FOUND LATER, ITS HANDS POINTED TO THE TIME THE FIRE STARTED.

84

With the Capitol ablaze, Lt. Pratt and his men marched across town and torched the White House. Next they broke into the Treasury Building. After a fruitless search for money, they piled up old records (some dating to the Revolutionary War) and set the place on fire.

AUG. 25, 1814 — THE BRITISH SET FIRE TO HOUSES, STABLES, AND ALMOST EVERY PUBLIC BUILDING IN WASHINGTON. THEY WERE ABOUT TO TORCH THE U.S. PATENT OFFICE AT BLODGETT'S HOTEL WHEN THE SUPERINTENDENT OF PATENTS INTERVENED.

STOP! THIS IS PRIVATE PROPERTY.

THE SUPERINTENDENT

TO BURN WHAT IS USEFUL TO ALL MANKIND WOULD BE AS BARBAROUS AS TO BURN THE ALEXANDRIA LIBRARY FOR WHICH THE TURKS HAVE BEEN CONDEMNED BY ALL ENLIGHTENED NATIONS.

MAJOR WATERS RELENTED.

I...AH... I'LL CHECK WITH MAJOR JONES.

MAJ. JONES AGREED WITH THE SUPERINTENDENT, SO THE PATENT OFFICE WAS THE ONLY GOVERNMENT BUILDING IN WASHINGTON NOT BURNED. THE MAN WHO SAVED IT WAS *SUPERINTENDENT* WILLIAM THORNTON, THE DESIGNER OF THE U.S. CAPITOL.

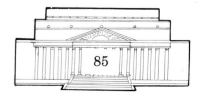

Many of the residents still in the city had sought refuge in St. Patrick's Church where Father William Matthews led them in prayer. Concerned for his safety, someone advised him to leave town. "Why should I leave," retorted the priest, "I have more business here now than ever before!"

WASHINGTON, D.C. WAS ABOUT TO BURN TO THE GROUND IN THE EARLY HOURS OF AUGUST 25, 1814. SUDDENLY A HEAVY RAIN FELL AND QUENCHED THE FIRE.

Rain and Rumors

AT DAWN HIGH WINDS BLEW DOWN SEVERAL HOUSES, KILLING THIRTY BRITISH SOLDIERS.

AT GREENLEAF'S POINT A DRY WELL CONTAINING GUNPOWDER EXPLODED, KILLING MORE BRITS.

THEN CAME RUMORS...

AMERICAN REINFORCEMENTS ARE CONVERGING ON THE CITY

THIS CHAIN OF EVENTS SHOOK BRITISH COMPOSURE, SO THE MOVED OUT, NEVER TO RETURN

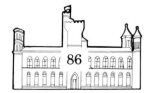

86

Following the burning of the Capitol, the House and Senate met in the only public building that remained undamaged, the Patent Office.

AFTER THE BRITISH BURNED WASHINGTON IN 1815 CONGRESS DISCUSSED MOVING THE CAPITAL SOME WHERE ELSE. LOCAL BUSINESSMEN BEGGED THEM TO STAY AND MADE AN IMPRESSIVE OFFER.

WE WILL ERECT A TEMPORARY BUILDING FOR YOU!

THE BRICK CAPITOL

THE TEMPORARY STRUCTURE, DUBBED *THE BRICK CAPITOL*, WAS COMPLETED LATE IN 1815. CONGRESS CONVENED THERE UNTIL 1819.

ON MARCH 4, 1817, **JAMES MONROE** TOOK THE OATH AS THE FIFTH PRESIDENT OF THE UNITED STATES IN FRONT OF THE *BRICK CAPITOL*. THIS WAS WASHINGTON'S **FIRST OUTDOOR INAUGURAL.**

THE SUPREME COURT BUILDING NOW STANDS ON THIS SITE.

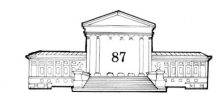

Confederate-run *Andersonville* has the legacy as the most horrible and inhumane prison of the Civil War, but most Yankee prisons fared no better. The Old Capitol Prison reeked with filth, lice, bedbugs, and spiders. Meals consisted of "half-spoiled beef and pork, half-cooked beans, and musty rice."

THE OLD CAPITOL PRISON

THE U.S. CAPITOL WAS AMONG THE BUILDINGS IN WASHINGTON TORCHED BY THE BRITISH DURING THE WAR OF 1812. CONGRESS QUICKLY APPROPRIATED FUNDS TO ERECT THIS BUILDING IN 1815 AT FIRST AND "A" STREETS. THE LAWMAKERS MET HERE UNTIL 1829.

WHEN CONGRESS MOVED BACK TO ITS PERMANENT LOCATION, THIS BUILDING BECAME KNOWN AS THE *OLD BRICK CAPITOL*.

BY THE OUTBREAK OF THE CIVIL WAR IN 1861 THE OLD CAPITOL WAS AN ABANDONED, DILAPIDATED MESS.

IT WILL MAKE AN **IDEAL PRISON** FOR CONFEDERATE OFFICERS, SPIES, BLOCKADE RUNNERS, AND SMUGGLERS!

ITS MOST FAMOUS INMATES WERE WOMEN SPIES INCLUDING ANTONIA FORD AND ROSE GREENHOW.

SHOWN HERE IS **BELLE BOYD** OF MARTINSBURG, VIRGINIA WHO TAUNTED HER GUARDS WITH INSULTS AND BY CONSTANTLY SINGING CONFEDERATE SONGS.

WELL, LOOKEE HERE. A BABOON WEARIN' A BLUE SUIT!

THE OLD CAPITOL PRISON WAS TORN DOWN IN 1932.

88

In an ironic twist, Heinrich Wirz, commandant of Anderson Prison, was confined at Old Capitol and hanged on a gallows in its yard.

The Statue of Freedom, as it is officially known, faces East. As a protection from lightning, ten bronze points tipped with platinum were placed on the statue: one on the head, six on the feathers in the headdress, one on each shoulder, and one on the shield.

The Lady on the Dome

AT NOON, DECEMBER 2, 1863, EVERY GUN IN THE TWELVE FORTS AROUND WASHINGTON, D.C. FIRED A SALUTE.

THE GRAND OCCASION WAS THE RAISING OF THE HEAD SECTION OF A STATUE 287 FEET TO THE TOP OF THE RECENTLY COMPLETED CAPITOL DOME.

WHEN IT WAS BOLTED TO ITS SHOULDERS, THE STATUE OF FREEDOM STOOD 19½ FT. HIGH AND WEIGHED SEVEN TONS.

VIRTUALLY FORGOTTEN IS THE DESIGNER OF THIS MONUMENT, AMERICA'S FIRST GREAT SCULPTOR, **THOMAS CRAWFORD** OF NEW YORK CITY.

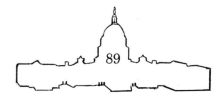

One of the earliest American sculptors was John Frazee. Born in 1790 in Rahway, NJ, he apprenticed to a bricklayer, but soon displayed a talent as a stone carver.

He moved to Greenwich Village and later founded the National Academy of Design. In 1831, he teamed up with Robert E. Launitz, a Latvian-born sculptor who studied with the great Thorvaldsen in Rome before moving to New York City.

THE ASPIRING SCULPTOR

Frazee and Launitz were teachers at the National Academy where they had a student who showed great promise. This is that student's story.

THOMAS CRAWFORD WAS BORN ON MARCH 22, 1813 IN MANHATTAN, THE SON OF **IRISH** IMMIGRANTS. BEFORE HE WAS TEN, THOMAS WAS DRAWING, PAINTING, AND CARVING FIGURES IN WOOD WITH A PEN KNIFE.

BUT IT WAS THE SIGHT OF STONE CUTTERS WORKING ON THE FACADES OF NEW BUILDINGS IN THE CITY THAT CONVINCED YOUNG CRAWFORD TO BECOME A SCULPTOR.

AT 19 HE ATTENDED THE NATIONAL ACADEMY OF DESIGN AT 23rd STREET AND 4th AVENUE. HE ALSO APPRENTICED AS A STONE CUTTER FOR JOHN FRAZEE AND ROBERT LAUNITZ.

FIGURING HE'D LEARN MORE IN EUROPE, THOMAS WENT TO ROME IN 1834 AT AGE 21, AND GOT A JOB COPYING STATUES FOR THE FAMOUS DANISH SCULPTOR ALBERT THORVALDSEN. THE PAY WAS LOUSY.

CRAWFORD LIVED IN POVERTY. NEVERTHELESS, HE KNOCKED OUT DOZENS OF STATUES IN HIS TINY APARTMENT WITHOUT EVER USING A MODEL.

CRAWFORD'S BREAK CAME IN 1839 WHEN HE MET A YOUNG, WEALTHY ATTORNEY NAMED CHARLES **SUMNER** WHO WAS TOURING EUROPE.

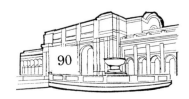

90

During the year he spent abroad (1839-40) Charles Sumner studied languages, history, and literature. He also met the leading pacifists of Europe who would greatly influence his philosophy as a future political leader of the United States.

SUMNER ALSO FORMED A LIFE-LONG FRIENDSHIP WITH THOMAS CRAWFORD, A STRUGGLING SCULPTOR WHO DID A MARBLE BUST OF THE BOSTONIAN'S PORTRAIT. SUMNER WAS SO IMPRESSED THAT, IN 1840...

HE OBTAINED A COMMISSION FOR THE 28 YEAR OLD SCULPTOR TO DO A STATUE OF *ORPHEUS AND CERBERUS.* WHEN IT WAS EXHIBITED AT THE BOSTON ATHENAEUM, THE ART CRITICS GAVE IT RAVE REVIEWS.

OVER THE NEXT DECADE, CRAWFORD WAS DELUGED WITH COMMISSIONS. HE COMPLETED THIS STATUE OF GEORGE WASHINGTON FOR THE CITY OF RICHMOND, VIRGINIA IN 1851.

MEANWHILE, SUMNER GOT ELECTED AS A U.S. SENATOR FROM MASSACHUSETTS. HE USED HIS INFLUENCE TO GET COMMISSIONS FOR HIS FRIEND IN ROME TO DO SCULPTURES FOR THE FEDERAL GOVERNMENT.

Charles Sumner was forty years old when he took his seat in the U.S. Senate in 1851 as a member of the Free Soil Party. A few years later he helped found the Republican Party. A firebrand orator, Sumner was staunchly opposed to slavery and secession.

He campaigned for civil service reforms and fought to give former slaves the right to vote. Not surprising, when the nation's capitol was being refurbished, Senator Sumner had some suggestions.

CAPITOL STATUARY

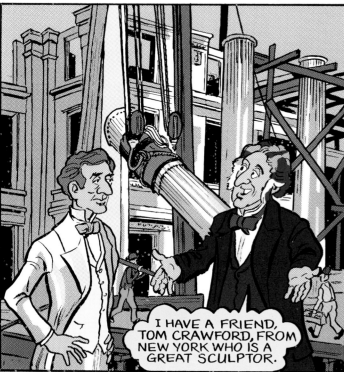

EXTENSIONS WERE ADDED TO THE EAST AND WEST WINGS OF THE U.S. CAPITOL IN WASHINGTON, D.C. IN THE 1850's. SECRETARY OF WAR JEFFERSON DAVIS WAS IN CHARGE OF THE WORK. ONE DAY HE WAS VISITED BY A SENATOR FROM MASSACHUSETTS — CHARLES SUMNER.

I HAVE A FRIEND, TOM CRAWFORD, FROM NEW YORK WHO IS A GREAT SCULPTOR.

HE'S CURRENTLY LIVING IN ROME. PERHAPS YOU CAN SEND HIM SOME WORK.

DAVIS TOOK THE HINT AND SENT A $20,000 CONTRACT TO CRAWFORD IN 1853.

TO FULFILL THE CONTRACT, CRAWFORD CREATED A PLASTER MODEL OF *THE PROGRESS OF CIVILIZATION*. HE SHIPPED IT TO WASHINGTON WHERE ANOTHER SCULPTOR CARVED IT IN MARBLE OVER THE EAST ENTRANCE TO THE U.S. SENATE.

DAVIS AND HIS BOSS, PRESIDENT FRANKLIN PIERCE, WERE SO IMPRESSED WITH CRAWFORD'S WORK THAT, IN 1855...

THEY PAID CRAWFORD $3,000 TO DESIGN THE *STATUE OF FREEDOM* FOR THE CAPITOL DOME.

HIS FIRST SKETCHES OF THE FIGURE CAUSED SECRETARY OF WAR JEFF DAVIS TO BLOW HIS TOP!

While Crawford was designing the *Statue of Freedom,* he went to Munich, Germany to work with Ferdinand von Muller on other pieces. These included a marble carving of *Adam and Eve* for the Boston Athenaeum and a ten-foot high statue of James Otis for Mount Auburn Cemetery. The majestic marble *Otis* is now at Harvard University.

 # Jeff Davis and the Lady's Hat

THOMAS CRAWFORD DREW SOME SKETCHES OF THE *STATUE OF FREEDOM* IN HIS STUDIO IN ROME. IN JULY, 1855 HE SENT THEM TO SECRETARY OF WAR JEFFERSON DAVIS FOR APPROVAL. INSTEAD, DAVIS HAD A FIT.

WHAT *IS* THIS?!

THAT CARVER FROM NEW YORK AND HIS FRIEND, SENATOR SUMNER, ARE TRYIN' T' PULL AN ABOLITIONIST PLOT!

THAT HAT USED T' BE WORN BY FREED SLAVES IN ANCIENT ROME. TELL CRAWFORD T' GET RID OF IT!

CRAWFORD GOT THE MESSAGE. THAT IS WHY THE STATUE ON THE CAPITOL DOME SPORTS A HELMET RINGED BY STARS AND TOPPED WITH A BALD EAGLE.

Clark Mills was born near Syracuse, New York on September 1, 1815. His father died when he was a boy, so he was sent to live with an uncle. He soon ran away because "Uncle" abused him.

With virtually no formal education, young Clark struck out on his own, picking up odd jobs and eventually drifting south to New Orleans.

By the age of twenty, Mills had worked as a carpenter, a millwright, and as a superintendent in a plaster and cement factory.

CLARK MILLS

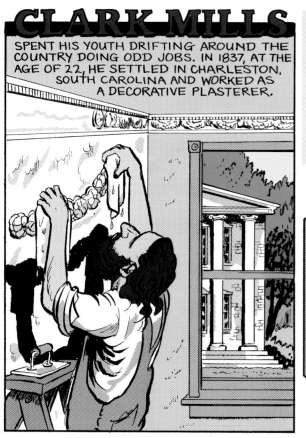

SPENT HIS YOUTH DRIFTING AROUND THE COUNTRY DOING ODD JOBS. IN 1837, AT THE AGE OF 22, HE SETTLED IN CHARLESTON, SOUTH CAROLINA AND WORKED AS A DECORATIVE PLASTERER.

AROUND 1840 HE TRIED HIS HAND AT MODELING PORTRAIT BUSTS IN CLAY. HIS RAW TALENT SOON ATTRACTED MANY CLIENTS.

IN 1845 HE SWITCHED TO MARBLE AND CHISELED A BUST OF SOUTH CAROLINA'S SENATOR (AND FORMER VICE-PRESIDENT OF THE U.S.) JOHN C. CALHOUN.

THEN, A GROUP OF WEALTHY GENTS AGREED TO BANKROLL MILLS' ART EDUCATION IN ROME, ITALY.

CHARLESTON'S CITY COUNCIL WAS SO IMPRESSED THAT THEY PURCHASED IT AND GAVE MR. MILLS A GOLD MEDAL.

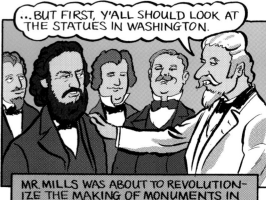

...BUT FIRST, Y'ALL SHOULD LOOK AT THE STATUES IN WASHINGTON.

MR. MILLS WAS ABOUT TO REVOLUTION-IZE THE MAKING OF MONUMENTS IN THE NATION'S CAPITAL.

The secret to Clark Mills' success as a portrait sculptor was a process he invented to make life masks in plaster. It caused the sitter much less discomfort than previous methods.

A COMMITTEE WAS ORGANIZED IN 1846 TO ERECT A MONUMENT TO THE LATE PRESIDENT ANDREW "OLD HICKORY" JACKSON IN WASHINGTON'S LAFAYETTE PARK. ITS CHAIRMAN WAS CAVE JOHNSON, THE POSTMASTER GENERAL.

I KNOW ABSOLUTELY NOTHING ABOUT SCULPTURE.

MEANWHILE, CLARK MILLS, AN UP AND COMING SCULPTOR, WAS VISITING WASHINGTON, D.C. A FRIEND OF SENATOR JOHN C. CALHOUN INTRODUCED MILLS TO MR. JOHNSON.

A SCULPTOR, EH? HOW'D YOU LIKE TO DO AN EQUESTRIAN STATUE OF ANDREW JACKSON?

A MAN ON HORSEBACK IS VERY DIFFICULT, EVEN FOR THE MOST EXPERIENCED SCULPTORS. I'M AFRAID I MUST DECLINE.

OLD HICKORY'S STATUE

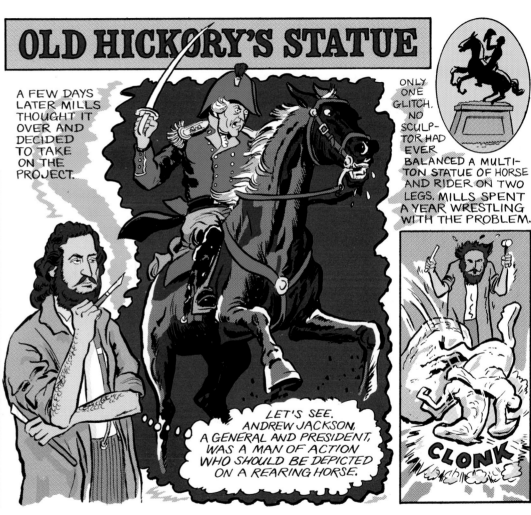

A FEW DAYS LATER MILLS THOUGHT IT OVER AND DECIDED TO TAKE ON THE PROJECT.

LET'S SEE. ANDREW JACKSON, A GENERAL AND PRESIDENT, WAS A MAN OF ACTION WHO SHOULD BE DEPICTED ON A REARING HORSE.

ONLY ONE GLITCH. NO SCULPTOR HAD EVER BALANCED A MULTI-TON STATUE OF HORSE AND RIDER ON TWO LEGS. MILLS SPENT A YEAR WRESTLING WITH THE PROBLEM.

CLONK

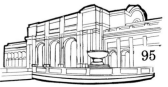

The challenge of balancing the entire weight of a horse and rider on the slender hind legs of the animal had stumped the likes of Leonardo da Vinci who failed doing a Sforza monument for Milan, Italy in the 16th century.

Another sculptor, Pietro Tacca in 1635 carved "Philip IV" on a rearing horse in the Plaza del Oriente in Madrid, Spain. However, ol' Pietro cheated by attaching the horse's tail to the back wall of the niche.

THE BRONZE CHALLENGE

CLARK MILLS COMPLETED A PLASTER MODEL OF ANDREW JACKSON'S STATUE FOR LAFAYETTE PARK IN MAY, 1850. THE MONUMENT COMMITTEE PROMPTLY AWARDED HIM A $12,000 COMMISSION TO PRODUCE IT IN **BRONZE.**

I BALANCED IT BY PLACING THE MAXIMUM WEIGHT OVER THE HIND HOOVES. THE RUMP IS HEAVIER THAN THE FOREPARTS.

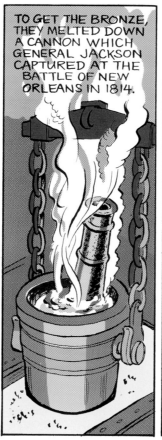

TO GET THE BRONZE, THEY MELTED DOWN A CANNON WHICH GENERAL JACKSON CAPTURED AT THE BATTLE OF NEW ORLEANS IN 1814.

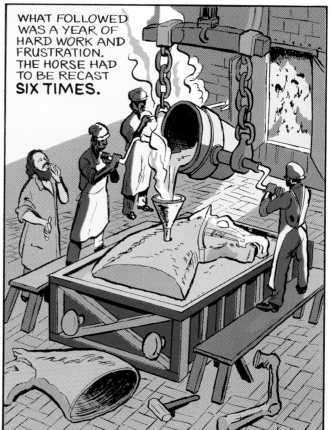

WHAT FOLLOWED WAS A YEAR OF HARD WORK AND FRUSTRATION. THE HORSE HAD TO BE RECAST **SIX TIMES.**

THE CRANE COLLAPSED...

KEE-RASH!

BOOM

AND THE FURNACE EXPLODED.

January 8th was selected as the unveiling date for the monument because it is the anniversary of General Andrew Jackson's victory over the British in the Battle of New Orleans in 1814.

CLARK MILLS FINALLY COMPLETED THE CASTING OF ANDREW JACKSON'S STATUE IN 1852. ON JANUARY 8, 1853, PRESIDENT MILLARD FILLMORE AND VIRTUALLY EVERY BIG SHOT IN WASHINGTON TURNED OUT FOR A MASSIVE PARADE TO LAFAYETTE PARK WHERE THE UNVEILING WAS TO TAKE PLACE.

THE UNVEILING GALA

AFTER A LONG-WINDED SPEECH BY STEPHEN DOUGLAS, MR. MILLS UNVEILED THE STATUE WITHOUT SAYING A WORD.

AFTER HEARING ABOUT ALL THE TROUBLE MILLS HAD IN CASTING THE SCULPTURE, CONGRESS VOTED TO GIVE HIM $20,000 ON TOP OF THE $12,000 HE HAD ALREADY RECEIVED.

CONSIDER IT A COST OVERRUN.

Aside from being an artistic and engineering marvel, the Andrew Jackson monument is important because it was the first equestrian statue created by an American-born sculptor.

CLARK MILLS MADE A SMALL FORTUNE ON STATUES OF ANDREW JACKSON. HE SOLD FULL-SIZE REPLICAS TO THE CITIES OF NEW ORLEANS, LOUISIANA AND NASHVILLE, TENNESSEE, ALONG WITH PLASTER STATUETTES TO PLACES LIKE THE MARYLAND HISTORICAL SOCIETY IN BALTIMORE. MOST OF THE CASTING AND FINISH WORK WAS DONE BY SLAVES.

NEXT, CONGRESS COMMISSIONED MILLS IN 1853 TO CREATE ANOTHER EQUESTRIAN SCULPTURE, THIS TIME OF GEORGE WASHINGTON. AS BEFORE, SLAVES DID MOST OF THE WORK.

PRESIDENT JAMES BUCHANAN UNVEILED IT ON OL' GEORGE'S BIRTHDAY, 1860 IN WASHINGTON CIRCLE ON PENNSYLVANIA AVE. AND 23rd ST. IN FOGGY BOTTOM.

STATUES BY SLAVES

MEANWHILE, MILLS BUILT THIS FOUNDRY IN BLADENSBURG, MARYLAND.

NEXT, MILLS SET HIS SIGHTS ON ANOTHER COMMISSION~ THE CASTING OF THOMAS CRAWFORD'S *STATUE OF FREEDOM* TO STAND ATOP THE DOME OF THE U.S. CAPITOL.

The Statue of Freedom is a female warrior clad in flowing draperies with her right hand resting on the hilt of a sheathed sword while her left hand holds a wreath and a shield. Holding her clothing together is a brooch on her waist with the inscription "U.S." Her helmet is encircled with stars topped by an eagle's head and a bold arrangement of feathers similar to an Indian's headdress.

THOMAS CRAWFORD COMPLETED A FULL-SIZE PLASTER MODEL OF THE *STATUE OF FREEDOM* AT HIS STUDIO IN ROME, ITALY IN 1856. WHEN CAST IN BRONZE, IT WOULD STAND ATOP THE DOME OF THE UNITED STATES CAPITOL.

A YEAR LATER, CRAWFORD DIED OF A BRAIN TUMOR. HIS BODY WAS BROUGHT TO BROOKLYN, NEW YORK FOR BURIAL IN GREENWOOD CEMETERY.

THE UNSINKABLE MODEL

IN APRIL, 1858, THE MODEL LEFT ROME IN SIX CRATES ABOARD THE *EMILY TAYLOR*.

WHILE CROSSING THE ATLANTIC, THE *TAYLOR* SPRUNG A LEAK WHICH GOT PROGRESSIVELY WORSE.

TO LIGHTEN THE LOAD AND SAVE THE VALUABLE SCULPTURE, THE CREW JETTISONED SOME OF THE CARGO.

THE *TAYLOR* MADE IT TO BERMUDA AND WAS CONDEMNED. *FREEDOM* WAS TRANSFERRED TO ANOTHER SHIP FOR THE TRIP TO MILLS' BRONZE FOUNDRY IN MARYLAND.

The U. S. Government paid Mr. Crawford $3,000 for his design of the *Statue of Freedom*.

It was two years before all sections reached the United States. Meanwhile, Clark Mills was lobbying for the commission to do the casting.

The War Department was responsible for renovating the U. S. Capitol, and John Floyd was the Secretary of War at the time. Clark Mills got the entire Congressional delegation from South Carolina, his home state, to call on Mr. Floyd. Floyd then opened negotiations between Mills and the govern-- ment. No competitive bids were ever sought.

THE FOUNDRY FOREMAN

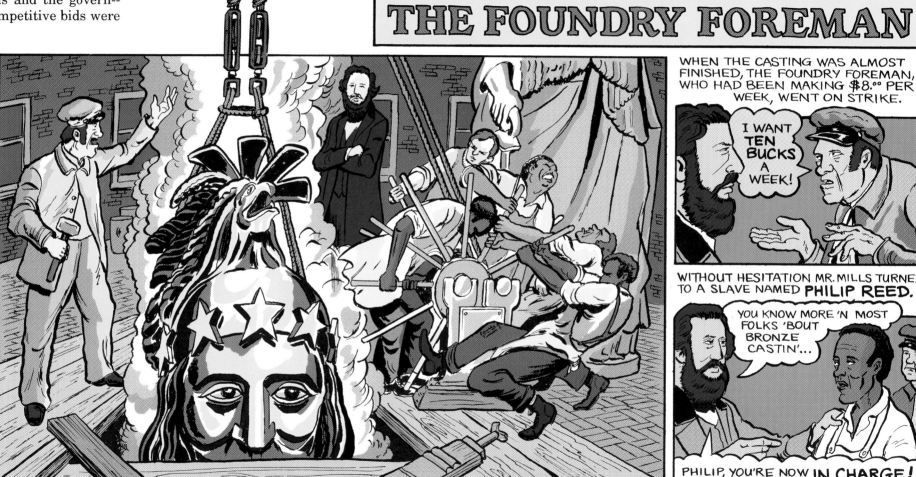

CLARK MILLS ORIGINALLY ASKED THE GOVERNMENT FOR $20,000 WITH $10,000 IN ADVANCE TO CAST THE *STATUE OF FREEDOM.*

THE FEDS SAID, "OUTRAGEOUS," SO MR. MILLS RELENTED.

A DEAL WAS STRUCK WHEREBY THE GOVERNMENT WOULD HIRE MILLS AND RENT HIS FOUNDRY IN BLADENSBURG, MD FOR $400 A MONTH.

WORK BEGAN IN MAY, 1860.

SHOWN HERE- HOISTING *FREEDOM'S* HEAD FROM THE BRONZE CASTING PIT.

WHEN THE CASTING WAS ALMOST FINISHED, THE FOUNDRY FOREMAN, WHO HAD BEEN MAKING $8.⁰⁰ PER WEEK, WENT ON STRIKE.

I WANT **TEN BUCKS** A WEEK!

WITHOUT HESITATION MR. MILLS TURNED TO A SLAVE NAMED **PHILIP REED.**

YOU KNOW MORE 'N MOST FOLKS 'BOUT BRONZE CASTIN'...

PHILIP, YOU'RE NOW **IN CHARGE!**

To make it easier to hoist the huge, cumbersome statue to the top of the Capitol dome, Clark Mills cast it in five sections, each weighing over a ton. The casting was finished in March, 1863.

Then, each section was loaded onto a heavy, reinforced wagon for the slow, laborious trip from Bladensburg, Maryland to the Capitol.

The government paid Mr. Mills about $23,736 for the material, casting, labor, and delivery.

THE STATUE OF FREEDOM

WAS PUT TOGETHER ON THE EAST GROUNDS OF THE CAPITOL BY PHILIP REED AND OTHER SLAVES IN THE SPRING OF 1863. THE PURPOSE WAS TO MAKE SURE ALL THE PIECES FIT TOGETHER PROPERLY.

THE STATUE WILL REMAIN ON DISPLAY HERE UNTIL THEY FINISH BUILDING THE ELABORATE PEDESTAL FOR HER ON TOP OF THE DOME.

It took Philip Reed 31 days to assemble *Freedom* for which he was paid $38.75. Slaves were sometimes paid cash for doing certain jobs even though, by law, they were somebody's "property." At the time, Mr. Reed was owned by Clark Mills.

A delegation called on President Lincoln and asked whether the material being used to complete the Capitol might be better used as sinews of war. Lincoln quickly shot back, "Work on the Capitol should go on as a symbol that the Union would go on!"

35-Gun Salute

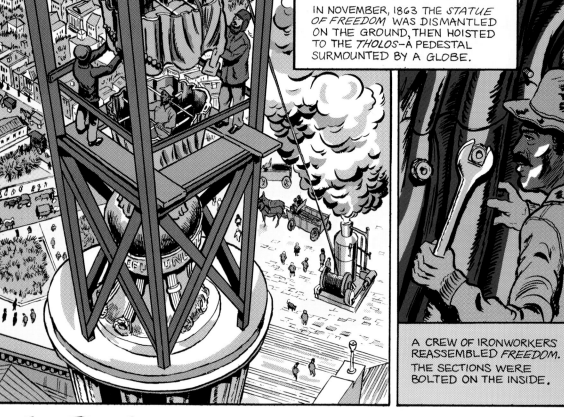

IN NOVEMBER, 1863 THE *STATUE OF FREEDOM* WAS DISMANTLED ON THE GROUND, THEN HOISTED TO THE *THOLOS*—A PEDESTAL SURMOUNTED BY A GLOBE.

CHARLES F. THOMAS, THE GOVERNMENT'S SUPERINTENDENT OF IRON WORK, HAD THE HONOR OF ATTACHING *FREEDOM'S* HEAD TO HER SHOULDERS ON DECEMBER 2, 1863.

A CREW OF IRONWORKERS REASSEMBLED *FREEDOM*. THE SECTIONS WERE BOLTED ON THE INSIDE.

AS A CROWD QUIETLY WATCHED MR. THOMAS PLACE A FLAG ON THE STATUE, THE TWELVE FORTS SURROUNDING WASHINGTON FIRED A 35-GUN SALUTE, ONE SHOT FOR EACH STATE IN THE UNION AT THE TIME INCLUDING THE CONFEDERATE STATES.

102

Epilog--One hundred thirty years later, in the spring of 1993, the *Statue of Freedom* was taken down from her pedestal and completely refurbished. She stood on the East Plaza of the Capitol for five months.

On October 23, 1993 she was carried back to her perch. Each time *Freedom* was lifted, the job was done by an S-64 Skycrane helicopter. The total cost of the scaffolding, helicopter, labor, material, etc. was about $750,000.

Index

About the Artist-Author

Patrick M. Reynolds is a graduate of Pratt Institute, Brooklyn, NY and holds a Masters of Fine Arts in Illustration from Syracuse University. A retired Lt. Colonel (Infantry) in the US Army Reserve, he served in the Vietnam War then taught Military History and other subjects in the Army Command and General Staff Officers Course.

Mr. Reynolds does all the research, writing and artwork for several illustrated history features that appear weekly in newspapers. He started in 1976 with **Pennsylvania Profiles** which ran in over thirty publications until 1991.

Currently he does three illustrated histories: **Texas Lore** for the *Dallas Morning News* and the *San Antonio Express-News,* **Big Apple Almanac**, about New York and Long Island for *Newsday*, and **Flashbacks** for the *Washington Post* and other newspapers. The stories in this book have been gleaned from **Flashbacks.**

Pennsylvania Profiles has been published in fifteen volumes. **Texas Lore** is a twelve-volume set. **Big Apple Almanac** is currently a collection of three full-color books.